Harvard Business Review

ON

CORPORATE

STRATEGY

D1531632

A HARVARD BUSINESS REVIEW PAPERBACK

The *Harvard Business Review* articles in this collection are avail-able as individual reprints. Discounts apply to quantity pur-chases. For information and ordering, please contact Customer Service, Harvard Business School Publishing, Boston, MA 02163. Telephone: (617) 496-1449, 8 A.M. to 6 P.M. Eastern Time, Mon-day through Friday. Fax: (617) 496-1029, 24 hours a day. E-mail: custserv@hbsp.harvard.edu.

Library of Congress Cataloging-in-Publication Data
Harvard business review on corporate strategy.
     p.   cm. — (Harvard business review paperback series)
    Includes index.
    ISBN 1-57851-142-9 (alk. paper)
    1. Strategic planning.   I. Series.
HD30.28.H3788 1999
658.4'012—dc21   99-18898
                                   CIP

The paper used in this publication meets the requirements of the American National Standard for Permanence of Paper for Printed Library Materials Z39.49-1984.

Contents

Harvard Business Review

ON

CORPORATE

STRATEGY

Creating Corporate Advantage

DAVID J. COLLIS AND

CYNTHIA A. MONTGOMERY

Executive Summary

WHAT DIFFERENTIATES truly great corporate strategies from the merely adequate? How can executives at the corporate level create tangible advantage for their business that makes the whole more than the sum of the parts?

This article presents a comprehensive framework for value creation in the multibusiness company. It addresses the most fundamental questions of corporate strategy: What businesses should a company be in? How should it coordinate activities across businesses? What role should the corporate office play? How should the corporation measure and control performance?

Through detailed case studies of Tyco International, Sharp, the Newell Company, and Saatchi and Saatchi, the authors demonstrate that the answers to all those

1

questions are driven largely by the nature of a company's special resources—its assets, skills, and capabilities. These range along a continuum from highly specialized at one end to the very general at the other. A corporation's location on the continuum constrains the set of businesses it should compete in and limits its choices about the design of its organization.

Applying the framework, the authors point out the common mistakes that result from misaligned corporate strategies. Companies mistakenly enter businesses based on similarities in products rather than the resources that contribute to the competitive advantage in each business. Instead of tailoring organizational structures and systems to the needs of a particular strategy, they create plain-vanilla corporate offices and infrastructures. The company examples demonstrate that one size does not fit all. One can find great corporate strategies all along the continuum.

MOST MULTIBUSINESS COMPANIES are the sum of their parts and nothing more. Although executives have become more sophisticated in their understanding of what it takes to achieve competitive advantage at the level of individual businesses, when it comes to creating *corporate* advantage across multiple businesses, the news is far less encouraging.

True, corporate executives face mounting pressure from their boards and from capital markets to add value. To date, however, that pressure has had the greatest impact on corporate strategy in pathological companies such as ITT, where the *destruction* of value was so great that it had to be stopped. What has slipped under the radar are those companies—the majority, we would argue—that don't destroy value at the corporate level, but neither do they create it.

That failure is not for lack of trying. Indeed, in many of the 50 companies we studied during a six-year research project, corporate executives were struggling to create viable corporate strategies. Some were working on their core competencies, others were restructuring their corporate portfolios, and still others were building learning organizations. In each case, executives were focusing on individual elements of corporate strategy: resources, businesses, or organization. What was missing was the insight that turns those elements into an integrated whole. That insight is the essence of corporate advantage—the way a company creates value through the configuration and coordination of its multibusiness activities. Ultimately, it is what differentiates truly great corporate strategies from the merely adequate.

Most executives create plain-vanilla corporate offices as if there were one best practice that every company should follow.

Choices Along the Resource Continuum

An outstanding corporate strategy is not a random collection of individual building blocks but a carefully constructed system of interdependent parts. More than a powerful idea, it actively directs executives' decisions about the resources the corporation will develop, the businesses the corporation will compete in, and the organization that will make it all come to life.

But there's more to it than that: in a great corporate strategy, all of these elements are aligned with one another. That alignment is driven by the nature of the firm's resources—its special assets, skills, and capabilities. The firm's resources are the unifying thread, the element that ultimately determines the others. (See the exhibit "The Triangle of Corporate Strategy.")

The resources that provide the basis for corporate advantage range along a continuum—from the highly

The Triangle of Corporate Strategy

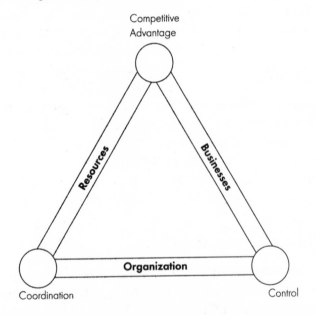

Great corporate strategies come in the first instance from strength in each side of the triangle: high-quality rather than pedestrian resources, strong market positions in attractive industries, and an efficient administrative organization. But true corporate advantage requires a tight fit at each angle as well. When a company's resources are critical to the success of its businesses, the result is competitive advantage. When the organization is configured to leverage those resources into the businesses, synergy can be captured and coordination achieved. Finally, fit between a company's measurement and reward systems and its businesses produces strategic control.

specialized at one end to the very general at the other. Sharp Corporation, the Japanese electronics company, has specialized technological expertise in optoelectronics that gives each of its businesses a competitive advantage. Tyco International, a conglomerate at the opposite end of the continuum, creates value for its businesses through a set of general management skills and a system of corporate governance. (See the exhibit "The Resource Continuum.")

This continuum of strategic resources is important because a corporation's location on the continuum constrains the set of businesses it should compete in and limits its choices about the design of its organization. Our research suggests that most executives think they're getting the alignment of their corporate strategies right, when in fact they are not. They mistakenly enter businesses based on similarities in products rather than similarities in the resources that contribute to competitive advantage in each business. It is a common—and costly—mistake. (See "Relatedness Is about Resources, Not Products" at the end of this article.) Moreover, instead of tailoring organizational structures and systems to the needs of a particular strategy, they create plain-vanilla corporate offices and infrastructures as if there were one best practice that every company should follow. The current fashion happens to favor a lean, minimalist corporate office—but, as we shall see, one size does not fit all.

Far from it. One can find great corporate strategies in companies all along the continuum. Some companies may fit the lean mode, while others require richer and deeper infrastructures. Consider the Newell Company, whose resources are neither exceedingly general nor specific but an attractive mixture of both.

The Resource Continuum

The resources that provide the basis for corporate advantage range along a continuum—from the highly specialized at one end to the very general at the other. A corporation's location on the continuum constrains the set of businesses it should compete in and limits its choices about the design of its organization along the other dimensions below.

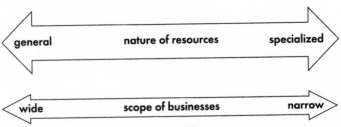

general   **nature of resources**   specialized

wide   **scope of businesses**   narrow

Companies with specialized resources will compete in a narrower range of businesses than companies with more general resources.

transferring   **coordination mechanisms**   sharing

The more general the resource, the more likely the company can effectively deploy it through transfer rather than sharing.

financial   **control systems**   operating

As resources become more specialized, the value of moving from financial to operating controls increases.

small   **corporate office size**   large

The more general the resources and the less the need for sharing, the smaller the corporate office should be.

Newell's Corporate Advantage

In 1966, Daniel Ferguson, a Stanford M.B.A., became CEO of Newell, an old-line manufacturer of brass curtain rods. The company had revenues of $14 million, a limited product line of drapery hardware, and no articulated strategy for the future. Ferguson began to develop a "build on what we do best" philosophy. At the time, Newell was selling extensively to Woolworth's and to Kresge (later Kmart). Ferguson foresaw the trend toward consolidation in the retail business and envisioned a role for Newell: "We realized we knew how to make a high-volume, low-cost product, and we knew how to relate to and sell to the large mass retailer."

In July 1967, Ferguson wrote out his strategy for Newell, identifying its focus as the market for hardware and do-it-yourself products. The company then made its first nondrapery hardware acquisition—Mirra-Cote, a producer of bath hardware—in order to gain access to new discount outlets for Newell's existing products. Over the next three decades, more than 75 acquisitions followed, all guided by Ferguson's carefully articulated strategy of 1967: "Newell defines its basic business as that of manufacturing and distributing volume merchandise lines to the volume merchandisers. A combination or package of lines going to the large retailers carries more marketing impact than each line separately, and Newell intends to build its growth through performance and marketing leverage of this package."

Although that strategy has been reviewed annually, its basic tenets have remained largely unchanged. Steadily pursuing this vision, Newell had sales of nearly $3 billion by 1997 and was ranked twenty-second on the

Fortune 500 in ten-year total return to shareholders. A review of Newell's corporate strategy reveals why.

RESOURCES AND BUSINESSES

Today the products Newell makes range from propane torches to hair barrettes to office products. That may appear to be a bizarre collection of unrelated items, yet Newell is far from being a conglomerate. The relatedness across its businesses comes not from similarities in the products themselves but from the common resources they draw on: Newell's relationships with discount retailers, its efficient high-volume manufacturing, and its superior service, including national coverage, on-time delivery, and program merchandising.

How do we know that Newell has the right balance of resources and businesses? Because the firm's corporate capabilities enhance the competitiveness of every business it owns. Many of the companies Newell has acquired were subpar performers. Under its ownership, typical operating margins have increased threefold, from about 5% to 15% or more.

The company's resources define the businesses that make sense for it to own and those that do not. Newell will never compete in high-tech, seasonal, or fashion products because they require skills the company doesn't have. Nor will it enter businesses whose dominant channel of distribution is outside discount retailing. Indeed, Newell sold off Wm. E. Wright, a profitable line of home sewing products, when its distribution shifted to specialty stores. This need for fit between resources and businesses constrains the set of businesses in which a company should operate but increases the likelihood that a multibusiness strategy will actually create value.

ORGANIZATION

A great corporate strategy begins with a vision of how a company's resources will differentiate it from competitors across multiple businesses. But it must also articulate how to achieve that vision. In particular, what kinds of coordination and control must the company provide in order to effectively deploy its resources?

Most corporate-level executives understand the need to add value to their businesses, yet few put in place the organizational mechanisms to make that possible. Many executives are reluctant to violate the autonomy and accountability of independent business units. Others fear they will end up with large, bureaucratic overhead structures. Companies like Newell, however, achieve the benefits of coordination with modest organizational costs.

Coordination. Newell understands that the outright sharing of resources such as a common sales force is not always the best way to capture synergies. So Newell *transfers* critical resources throughout the firm without undermining the independence of its business units. (See "Should Corporate Resources Be Shared or Transferred?" at the end of this article.)

Much of Newell's know-how and experience is embedded in its managers. To leverage that resource, Newell deliberately moves managers across business units and from the business to the corporate level. That practice enables Newell to transfer experience and to build a skilled in-house labor pool. Job openings are publicized widely within the company and usually are filled by in-house candidates. For Newell, the benefits of such transfers can be fully realized because of the commonalities across its businesses—and that is not an accident but a result of forethought.

Other transfers of learning occur when divisional leaders convene six times a year for presidents' meetings and when they meet one another at trade shows. Annual management meetings bring together functional vice presidents for sales and marketing, operations, personnel, control, and customer service from all divisions. Each functional group has its own two-day meeting, featuring presentations and programs aimed at transferring best practices across the divisions.

In contrast to its many resource transfers, the only activity Newell *shares* among its businesses is its advanced data-management system. Meeting the needs of its demanding customers for efficient logistics, billing, and collection is so central to Newell's strategy—and the activity is so scale sensitive—that the corporate office itself takes responsibility for those tasks and requires the divisions to accept its terms and conditions. All other operational activities, including sales, are the responsibility of Newell's 20 independent divisions. The company explicitly chose not to form one central sales force, fearing the consequences of lost autonomy and accountability at the business level.

Control Systems. The other element of infra-structure that plays an important role in corporate strategy is a firm's control systems. Without the appropriate control systems, the corporate center can quickly lose its ability to determine strategic direction and influence performance in the individual businesses. That is why choices about what to measure and reward are so important. Broadly speaking, corporations have the choice between two types of control systems: operating or financial.

Understanding which one fits a company's particular resources and businesses is critical to creating corporate advantage. (See "Financial versus Operating Control" at the end of this article.)

Newell's system of operating controls fits its strategy of leveraging the experience of senior managers. The system focuses on 30 operating variables that management believes are critical to the success of the businesses—and because the businesses have so many similarities, a single carefully tailored system can be applied to all of them.

For example, regardless of how a business unit is organized, Newell believes its SG&A expenses should never exceed 15%. All variances are bracketed, and too many variances lead to a "brackets meeting." Similarly, even if sales are above budget, managers will intervene if the fixed-cost numbers show an unfavorable variance. Senior managers are intimately involved in the oversight and monitoring of the businesses, principally through monthly performance reviews that allow them to add value in discussions with divisional managers.

Compensation systems are always central to control systems. Again, Newell's is aligned with its strategy. To facilitate transfers, compensation is uniform across divisions; base salaries are determined by position and division size. Newell holds individual managers and operating units accountable for performance, and it rewards excellence. Managers who make it over Newell's high hurdle for bonus payouts—by achieving at least a 32.5% return on assets—are handsomely rewarded for their efforts with bonuses of up to 100% of their base compensation.

Corporate Office. A thoughtful observer would understand Newell's corporate strategy by walking around its headquarters and noting who was there and what they were doing—a simple mirror of any strategy. In 1997, there were 375 people on Newell's corporate staff. Beyond a small cadre of highly experienced senior managers who interacted frequently with the business heads, most of those people worked on the company's centralized data-management systems, which were critical to the company's operations.

From the top down, Newell maintains a culture deeply permeated by the expectation that it will be a leader in serving the needs of discount retailers. It is a source of pride that a frequently asked question in the industry is, "Do you ship as well as Newell?" Nearly all of Newell's senior managers maintain high-level relationships with customers, not to sell a particular product but to "sell Newell." As Daniel Ferguson explains, "Like everything else we do in marketing to the mass retailer, the more they see us as an effective partner, the greater the edge we have when a certain product comes up for review."

For all the value Newell adds to its businesses, it levies a corporate charge of only 2% of sales, a number far below the increase in operating margins the divisions gain by being part of Newell. That sort of tangible value has enabled Newell to achieve a ten-year total return to investors of 31% per year, compared with an 18% average for the S&P 500.

The Lessons of Newell

What are the most important lessons of Newell's long-term success?

- First, corporate strategy is guided by a vision of how a firm, as a whole, will create value. When Daniel

Ferguson first laid out Newell's strategy, the company's resources were modest at best. Ferguson made the commitment to invest in and build the resources that allowed Newell to compete in a changing market.

- Second, corporate strategy is a system of interdependent parts. Its success depends not only on the quality of the individual elements but also on how the elements reinforce one another.

- Third, corporate strategy must be consistent with, and capitalize on, opportunities outside the company. Newell caught the upswing in discount retailing 30 years ago; more recently, it adjusted its domestic focus to exploit the growth of other "category killers" such as Home Depot and the office products superstores.

- Fourth, the benefits of corporate membership must be greater than the costs. Most corporate advantages are realized in the enhanced performance of the business units. While better performance is often more difficult to measure than in Newell's case, corporations must determine if they are achieving it. If they are not, they are not creating real corporate advantage.

Looking closely at how the elements of Newell's strategy work as a system, we see that its resources are the unifying thread. It is the nature of Newell's resources that determines the businesses it should compete in, the design of Newell's organization, and the role the corporate office should play in the coordination and control of its businesses.

Sharing Resources at Sharp

Sharp Corporation, a $14 billion consumer-electronics giant, sits near the specialized end of the resource continuum. Seen at one time as a second-tier competitor by its Japanese rivals, Sharp's consistent pursuit of a vision of technological creativity has pushed it to the forefront of its industry.

RESOURCES AND BUSINESSES

Sharp's valuable resources are a set of specialized optoelectronics technologies that contributes to the competitive advantage of the company's core businesses. Its most successful technology has been liquid crystal displays (LCDs), which are critical components in nearly all Sharp's products. The competitive advantage this resource confers is illustrated by Sharp's success in video recorders. Its breakthrough Viewcam was the first to incorporate an LCD viewfinder, an innovation that propelled Sharp to capture 20% of the Japanese market within six months of the product's introduction.

Atsushi Asada, a Sharp senior executive, described Sharp's technology strategy: "We invest in the technologies that will be the nucleus of the company in the future. Like a nucleus, such technologies should have an explosive power to multiply themselves across many products." By following this strategy, Sharp can successfully extend its scope into many new businesses, as long as competitive advantage in those businesses depends on one of its core technologies. For example, as an extension of its screen technology, Sharp created the personal electronic organizer with its Wizard product.

Like most companies that operate near the specialized end of the resource spectrum, Sharp's set of businesses is fairly restricted: television and video systems, communications and audio systems, appliances, information systems, and electronic components. Unlike its competitors Sony and Matsushita, Sharp has never considered entering the movie business because it knows it has no competitive advantage outside its technology base.

ORGANIZATION

Sharp's technological investments share several characteristics: they tend to be expensive, they often have substantial lead times, and the advantages they confer in products may be short-lived because of imitation or brief life cycles. To be successful in such an environment, Sharp must make good investment choices and, to recoup its investment, it must leverage new technologies quickly and broadly throughout the company.

Hence Sharp has a corporate office, not counting corporate R&D, of more than 1,500 people. Judged by today's fashion for lean corporate staff, that number is bound to appear shockingly large. Sharp's strategy, however, depends critically on extensive, intricate coordination of its shared technological activities—thus the logic behind its headquarters staffing. (See the exhibit "How Big Should a Corporate Office Be? One Size Does Not Fit All.")

Coordination. The need to share activities determines Sharp's basic structure. Unlike Newell, Sharp is divided into functional units, not product divisions. As a result, applied research and manufacturing of key components, such as LCDs, occur in a single specialized unit where scale economies can be exploited. In contrast, Honeywell, a typical U.S. company organized by product divisions, at one time had LCD research activity in seven divisions.

To prevent the functional groups from becoming vertical chimneys that obstruct effective product development, Sharp employs product managers who have responsibility—but not authority—for coordinating the entire set of value chain activities. And the company convenes enormous numbers of cross-unit and corporate committees to ensure that shared activities, including the corporate R&D unit and sales forces, are optimally configured and allocated among the different product lines. Sharp invests in such time-intensive coor-

How Big Should a Corporate Office Be? One Size Does Not Fit All.

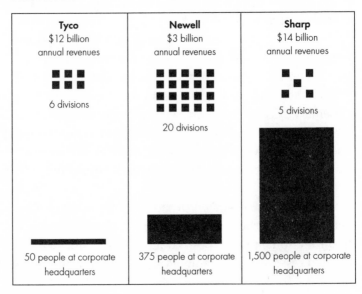

Tyco $12 billion annual revenues	Newell $3 billion annual revenues	Sharp $14 billion annual revenues
6 divisions	20 divisions	5 divisions
50 people at corporate headquarters	375 people at corporate headquarters	1,500 people at corporate headquarters

dination to minimize the inevitable conflicts that arise when units share important activities.

Each year, nearly one-third of Sharp's corporate R&D budget is spent on 10 to 15 Gold Badge projects. These are selected at the corporate technical strategy meeting because they involve original technologies that cut across product groups. All project members are vested with the authority of the company president and wear his gold-colored badge so that they can call on people throughout Sharp for assistance.

Sharp has to employ an operating control system that focuses more on how people behave than on short-term financial outcomes.

Control Systems.   Because of the blurred accountability that results from its functional structure, Sharp requires a very different control system than a simple divisional P&L. It has to employ an operating control system that focuses more on how people behave than on the short-term financial outcomes they achieve. Promotion, therefore, rather than annual compensation, is the most powerful incentive, and employees are promoted on the basis of seniority and subtle skills exhibited over time, such as teamwork and communication. In a technologically based company with a functional organization structure, this control system is one of the few that will not unduly reward a short-term, self-interested orientation.

Like many Japanese companies, Sharp's culture reinforces the view that the company is a family or community whose members should cooperate for the greater good. In accordance with the policy of lifetime employment, turnover is very low, which encourages employees to accommodate everyone's interests and to pursue what's best for the company overall. That common outlook reduces the inevitable conflict over sharing such important resources as R&D and component manufacturing.

Like Newell, Sharp is successful in leveraging resources throughout its organization but, consistent with the nature of its underlying resources, it does so in very different ways. Newell's resources can be nurtured and transferred without confronting costly trade-offs across businesses. Merchandising practices used in one unit do not alter their use in another unit, and the development or deployment of those practices does not require extensive, coordinated decision making.

In contrast, Sharp's resources put greater demands on the organization. Their greatest benefits are realized when individual units collaborate and pool investments. In such a context, conflicts and trade-offs are inevitable; managing them well is critical to the success of strategies at that end of the resource continuum.

Controls and Incentives at Tyco

Tyco International represents the other end of the continuum from Sharp. Tyco is a $12 billion conglomerate built around a set of very general resources that it leverages into a wide range of businesses. Contrary to the widely held negative view of conglomerates, Tyco illustrates that a carefully conceived and implemented strategy at the far left of the continuum *can* create substantial amounts of value—even in the United States, and even in the late 1990s. Since 1993, the market capitalization of Tyco has grown from $1.2 billion to $25 billion. Return on equity in 1996 was 16%.

RESOURCES AND BUSINESSES

"What's special about Tyco," says CEO Dennis Kozlowski, "are its financial controls, good incentive programs, strong manufacturing, and operating managers who are highly motivated by incentives and who enjoy working without a whole lot of group support." Tyco's resources are general, much like those of venture capitalists and private equity groups.

Due to the broad applicability of their resources, companies like Tyco can operate in a wide range of businesses. In 1997, the company was organized around six operating groups: fire protection, flow control, disposable medical products, Simplex Technologies, packaging materials, and specialty products. Each of these independent product groups was headed by a president who reported directly to Kozlowski.

While there are few product similarities across Tyco's businesses, its resources—financial controls and governance structure—do set limits on the kinds of businesses it can own. Tyco confines itself to businesses in which division executives can be held strictly accountable for a limited number of financial measures. As a result, Tyco competes in mature, stable, low-tech businesses, which, compared with Sharp's, face less uncertainty and require considerably lower levels of R&D spending. Tyco could not succeed in high-tech businesses where external events can badly distort a year's financial results.

ORGANIZATION

Rather than reaching for specific synergies *across* its groups, Tyco uses the general resources of the corpora-

tion to encourage the division presidents to act like
entrepreneurs *within* their groups, and to focus on
expanding the scope and
Tyco's "no meetings, profitability of those units. As
no memos" philosophy Kozlowski explained several
is consistent with years ago, "While they have
the company's the backing of an old-line,
corporate strategy. financially secure, capable
company, they can act like
small entrepreneurs who go out and do what needs
to be done without all the encumbrances of the
corporation."[1]

A Tyco executive once likened the company's structure to a capitalistic system with "very little central
planning. We don't tend to set up a lot of rules. We
develop incentives for our people, and it works."[2] Indeed,
its highly disciplined financial-control system and steep
incentive schemes are at the heart of Tyco's strategy.

Tyco's managers are on the line to perform. The company's unsparing, top-down budgeting process holds
divisional presidents accountable for the financial performance of their individual units—and only for that. At
the same time, Tyco offers powerful incentives to
achieve extraordinary results, of which there have been
many. There is no cap on the bonuses for individual performance. In some cases, division heads make more
money than Tyco's CEO. When a manager fails to perform, Tyco will look for a replacement with relevant
industry expertise outside the organization. Because of
the wide scope of its businesses, it cannot draw from an
extensive internal labor pool the way Newell can.

Tyco recognizes that if you don't intend to achieve a
lot of coordination across your businesses, you shouldn't
have much of a corporate staff. That thinking is consis-

tent with Tyco's "no meetings, no memos" philosophy. In 1997, only 50 of the company's 40,000 employees were on the corporate staff. Its headquarters was in a modest frame building in New Hampshire. Like the rest of the corporate infrastructure, it was unpretentious but more than adequate to get the job done.

Kozlowski is aware of the criticisms of conglomerates and of the risks and challenges of holding a company together around a very general set of resources. He explains, "At least once a year we bring in someone from the outside who has a lot of incentive to break up the company—someone from a JP Morgan, Merrill Lynch, or Goldman Sachs—and say to them, 'take a good look at us, break us up, and tell us what we're going to get per share for it. Then tell us if you think we should break up.' It's the only way to get an objective look at it. And they've always said that we should stay as we are." Given Tyco's impressive record of value creation, it's not a surprising conclusion.

No One Right Strategy

When we look across the spectrum of resources—from Sharp's specialized technological expertise to Tyco's general management disciplines—one thing is clear: as brilliant as any one strategy might be, it won't necessarily work well for all companies. That's because every company starts at a different point, operates in a different context, and has fundamentally different kinds of resources. There is no best prescription for all multibusiness corporations. (See the exhibit "Three Well-Aligned Strategies.")

What prevails instead is the logic of internally consistent corporate strategies tailored to a firm's resources and opportunities. When corporate strategy adheres to this logic, a company can create a meaningful corporate advantage. When a strategy departs from it, a company at best will coast to mediocrity. At worst, the lack of consistency could be the iceberg that sinks the corporate ship. Consider the failure of Saatchi and Saatchi—at one time the world's largest advertising agency and now, renamed Cordiant, a shadow of its former self.

Saatchi and Saatchi rose to fame in the 1970s and early 1980s on its reputation for creative advertising and its championing of global advertisements. Those skills enabled it to build a client base that became its most valuable resource. In 1986, with the acquisition of Ted Bates, Saatchi became the world's largest advertising agency.

Three Well-Aligned Strategies

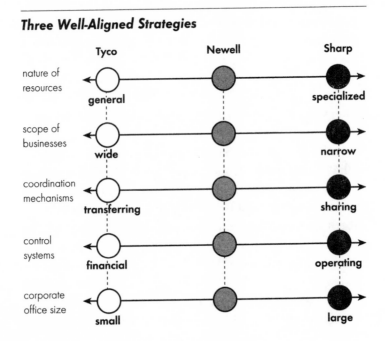

Within six years, the firm was on the verge of bankruptcy. Saatchi and Saatchi made many mistakes, including overpaying for acquisitions and not anticipating the end of the 1980s advertising boom. Its fate, however, was sealed by its failure to craft a coherent corporate strategy. Indeed, the company violated most of the requirements for internal alignment.

The vision for Saatchi was to be number one in its industry. However, unlike Newell or Sharp, Saatchi never established a boundary to its domain. Having reached the limit in advertising (where conflict of interest prevents one agency from becoming too large), Saatchi expanded into a number of businesses in which its relationship with a client's marketing executives provided a potential competitive advantage: marketing services, public relations, direct marketing, and promotions firms. But when Saatchi acquired consulting firms and then bid for a British merchant bank and a commercial bank, the client relationship was no longer a valuable resource. A marketing vice president is not the buyer of logistics consulting or banking services. Indeed, a corporate reputation for edgy creativity is probably the last thing a company looks for in its choice of commercial banker.

Worse still, even where there was potential synergy, Saatchi never implemented effective processes to capture it. Cross-selling was restricted to informational meetings where each business informed the others about its services, and no financial incentives were provided for referrals. The risk of a sister company souring a relationship inhibited businesses from sharing clients. As a result, Saatchi was never able to leverage its most valuable resource—customer relationships— across businesses.

But perhaps the worst failure came on the control side. Saatchi had developed what at the time was an advanced financial-control system for advertising agencies. But when an ex-consultant was placed in charge of both the consulting and the advertising businesses, he imposed the budgeting system from consulting on the advertising agencies. The consulting system starts not with expected client revenues, which are relatively predictable, but with desired numbers of employees. In consulting, where professionals by and large generate their own revenues, this is an adequate system. In the notoriously optimistic advertising business, it was a disaster. Agencies projected rapid growth in employees and acquired long-term leases on the office space to accommodate them. When the dust settled, Saatchi took write-offs of more than £150 million just to cover the excess floor space the company had leased. Saatchi's failure to understand the control requirements of different businesses undercut the enterprise.

Many Ways to Succeed

The fact that there are potentially an unlimited variety of effective corporate strategies does not mean that most corporate strategies are effective. Observation suggests the opposite—that many strategies do not enhance value. If executives benchmarked their corporate strategies as aggressively as they do their operations, most would discover that their strategies are far from world class.

The resource continuum and the range of strategies it encompasses provides a useful starting point for benchmarking the effectiveness of your corporate strategy. Begin by looking for companies with successful strategies built around types of resources that are similar to yours. Those companies can serve as models, while companies further away on the resource continuum can provide instructive contrasts.

The harsh moment of truth for many companies built around specialized resources comes when they discover that, despite the related appearance of their businesses, they are adding little more value to their businesses than a well-run conglomerate would. The performance of these companies, however, suffers from the drag of a larger corporate overhead than that of a conglomerate.

The acid test for any corporate strategy is this: the company's business must not be worth more to another owner.

At the other end of the spectrum, conglomerates often find that leveraged buyout firms have even lower-cost operations and more effective means for financing and controlling sets of unrelated businesses. Alternatively, conglomerates may discover that the businesses they own could be worth more in the hands of a corporation with more specialized resources.

That is the acid test for any corporate strategy: the company's businesses must not be worth more to another owner. In a dynamic, competitive environment, that threat is always lurking around the corner. To guard against it requires the continual upgrading not only of the resources on which the strategy is based but also of all the elements of the strategy triangle and their fit.

Newell, Sharp, and Tyco have all sustained corporate advantage over many years through just such a process of continual upgrading. Newell, for example, used to be proud of service levels that it would shun today. Tyco has ratcheted up the size of the acquisitions it is capable of making. Sharp has consciously fostered a feeling of crisis in the firm, a sense that the roof is falling in. Today, to respond to increased competition in some of its core markets, Sharp must be able to make another round of technology investments. The race never ends. But no company's strategy can endure without continual pressure to improve.

There are many ways to succeed. Creativity and intuition are hallmarks of great corporate strategies. So too, however, are discipline and rigor. In the companies we studied, brilliant strategies began with new ideas. These were followed by deliberate investments in resources made over many years, the development of a clear understanding of the businesses in which those resources would be valuable, and the painstaking tailoring of organizations to make the strategy a reality. Ultimately, strategies that prevail are well-constructed systems that deliver tangible benefits.

Relatedness Is about Resources, Not Products

MERCURY MEASURES—an actual company whose name has been disguised—makes industrial thermostats. Not long ago, growth prospects in its core markets had flattened. But not all was bleak. Mercury's head of marketing was forecasting strong growth in the demand for household thermostats. For Mercury's management team, pursuing such a natural extension of the company's current business was a no-brainer.

Three years and lots of red ink later, Mercury had to

write off the business. Why? At first glance, the strategy had made good sense. Mercury would remain a thermostat producer, adding only an additional product line. But a more careful and more rigorous look reveals that the fit between the two businesses was not at all close.

Mercury had all the factors needed for success in industrial thermostats: strong R&D capabilities; expertise in strict tolerance, made-to-order production; and a technically sophisticated sales force of industrial engineers. Although Mercury was able to leverage some of its technological know-how when it entered the household market, R&D was not critical for success in that market, nor did it constitute a significant portion of the added value.

Moreover, Mercury lacked the resources necessary to be competitive in household thermostats. It had no expertise in design, product appearance, or packaging; it lacked the capabilities for mass production; and it didn't know how to distribute products through industry representatives to mass marketers and contractors.

Like Mercury, companies often err by expanding into market segments that appear to be related to their existing businesses but in fact are quite different. In particular, they tend to make this mistake when they define relatedness according to product characteristics rather than resources.

Should Corporate Resources Be Shared or Transferred?

DEPLOYING KEY RESOURCES where they are important to the competitive advantage of individual businesses is at the heart of corporate strategy. Sometimes it makes sense for businesses to share a common resource, like a sales force or an MIS system. In other cases, resources can be transferred across businesses with a minimum of coordination. Knowing whether to transfer or share resources—and which mechanisms to use—is largely a question of what kind of resource you are trying to leverage.

A useful distinction can be made between resources that we call *public goods* and those we call *private goods*. By public goods, we mean, for example, brand names or best demonstrated practices—things that can be used in several businesses simultaneously without conflict. By private goods, we mean such things as a common sales force or component-manufacturing facility—resources that are much more difficult to manage and can lead to competition and conflicts between businesses.

Transferring public goods within a company can usually be done at arm's length with little intervention and coordination by the corporate office. Indeed, it may involve few, if any, explicit organizational mechanisms. For example, simply placing the Nike brand on a new line of sporting goods may convey a substantial competitive advantage to the business with relatively little effort on the part of the corporation. Other transfers can occur through occasional cross-business meetings and limited exchanges of information. When Disney introduces a new animated cartoon character, such as Hercules, the various Disney business units, from consumer products to theme parks, just need to be aware of one another's activities so that they don't conflict. Even the transfer of best practices, such as Newell's skills in inventory management and program merchandising, can be relatively straightforward. Experienced managers can move to the new division or a project team can act as consultants. Because there is no conflict in their use, and because even autonomous business units will actively seek to capitalize on such truly valuable corporate resources, transferring public goods can be done with relative ease, once the means for doing so are in place.

With public goods, the challenge is often in their development and preservation. Who should be responsible for the resource? How can you ensure that the necessary investments are being made? Should new practices be developed by the corporate office or allowed to flourish in many divisions before the best one is applied everywhere? It is also important to safeguard the use of some public goods, particularly intangible ones such as brand names or sets of relationships, so that one unit does not spoil or devalue the asset.

Private goods require more explicit coordination because the same resource is shared by multiple businesses and therefore its use by one unit can affect its use by another. Consider a corporate unit that buys materials for all divisions in order to exploit economies of scale in purchasing. Should Pepsico's three restaurants, Taco Bell, Pizza Hut, and KFC—recently spun off as Tricon Global Restaurants—jointly purchase toilet paper? If they did, they would save several hundred thousand dollars per year. Believe it or not, this simple decision took more than a year to resolve. One chain wanted one-ply tissue, another wanted two-ply, and the third did not care. This example is powerful precisely because it is so trivial. If it takes a year to reach a compromise agreement on a question like this, imagine how difficult and time consuming it can be to reach consensus on sharing something important, like a sales force.

Financial versus Operating Control

THERE ARE TWO fundamentally different methods for monitoring and controlling the performance of subordinates and business units. The first, *financial control*, holds managers accountable for a limited number of objective output measures, such as return on assets or aggregate sales growth. The second, *operating control*, recognizes that all sorts of events outside managers' influence, such as the bankruptcy of a major customer, may affect their performance. Rather than measuring outputs, operating control is concerned with evaluating managers' decisions and actions. Thus after an unexpected recession, financial control would punish managers because profit was below budget, while operating control might reward them for anticipating the downturn and cutting inventories, even though they missed their budget targets.

While most companies use some mix of the two, successful corporate strategies tend to emphasize one or the other. That choice depends primarily on the nature of the businesses in the portfolio and the relative expertise of corporate executives.

Financial control is most appropriate in mature, stable industries and for discrete business units. For such businesses, a few financial variables accurately reflect their strategic positions. In fast-moving industries with high levels of uncertainty, financial control is less suitable. In high-tech businesses, for example, current financial results may not capture the loss of technological leadership. Such measures may also be problematic when results across units are interdependent.

Operating control typically involves both quantitative

and qualitative assessments that capture the nuances of a particular business. To use operating control effectively, corporate managers have to be very familiar with the businesses in the firm's portfolio. Often the managers themselves will have extensive relevant operating experience.

Corporate managers may monitor dozens of line items such as reject rates, delivery lead times, and conversion statistics to assess the health of a business. The tradeoffs among the targets may not be fully specified and the evaluation and incentive schemes may resemble more an implicit contract than a simple objective target.

Operating control systems require far more interaction between corporate and business unit managers. Through frequent strategic-planning sessions, operating reviews, and capital-budgeting discussions, corporate management can closely observe managers' performance and act as coaches and sounding boards. Not surprisingly, such systems place more demands on an organization and generally lead to somewhat larger corporate infrastructures.

In contrast, financial control systems are the easiest to implement and place the fewest demands on corporate management. The key is to establish discrete business units, to hold management accountable for outcomes, and to provide strong incentives for managers to meet their numbers. The archetype of such systems is the LBO, in which financial targets not only are agreed to within the firm but also are bound by covenants with external providers of capital.

No control system can be assessed in isolation. Rather, its effectiveness depends on its degree of fit with the company's particular set of resources and businesses.

Notes

1. Mark McLaughlin, "Flat and Happy at the Top," *New England Business,* March 1990, p. 19.

2. "John Fort: CEO, Tyco Laboratories," *The Business of New Hampshire,* February 1997, p. 38.

Originally published in May–June 1998
Reprint 98303

Competing on Resources

Strategy in the 1990s

DAVID J. COLLIS AND
CYNTHIA A. MONTGOMERY

Executive Summary

HOW DO YOU CREATE and sustain a profitable strategy? Many of the approaches to strategy that have been championed in the past decade have focused the attention of managers inward, urging them to build a unique set of resources and capabilities. In practice, however, notions like core competence have too often become a "feel good" exercise that no one fails. The authors explain how a company's resources drive its performance in a dynamic competitive environment, and they propose a new framework that moves strategic thinking forward in two ways: (1) by laying out a pragmatic and rigorous set of market tests to determine whether a company's resources are truly valuable enough to serve as the basis for strategy; and (2) by integrating this market view of capabilities with earlier insights about competition and industry structure. Where a company chooses to play will determine its profitability as much as its resources.

The authors explain in clear managerial terms why some competitors are more profitable than others, how to put the idea of core competence into practice, and how to develop diversification strategies that make sense. Case examples such as Disney, Cooper, Sharp, and Newell illustrate the power of resource-based strategies. The authors show how these organizations have been able to use corporate resources to establish and maintain competitive advantage at the business-unit level, and also how they have benefited from the attractiveness of the markets in which they have chosen to compete.

As RECENTLY AS TEN YEARS AGO, we thought we knew most of what we needed to know about strategy. Portfolio planning, the experience curve, PIMS, Porter's five forces—tools like these brought rigor and legitimacy to strategy at both the business-unit and the corporate level. Leading companies, such as General Electric, built large staffs that reflected growing confidence in the value of strategic planning. Strategy consulting boutiques expanded rapidly and achieved widespread recognition. How different the landscape looks today. The armies of planners have all but disappeared, swept away by the turbulence of the past decade. On multiple fronts, strategy has come under fire.

At the business-unit level, the pace of global competition and technological change has left managers struggling to keep up. As markets move faster and faster, managers complain that strategic planning is too static and too slow. Strategy has also become deeply problematic at the corporate level. In the 1980s, it turned out that corporations were often destroying value by owning the very divisions that had seemed to fit so nicely in their growth/share matrices. Threatened by smaller, less hierarchical competitors, many corporate stalwarts either suffered devastating setbacks (IBM, Digital, General Motors, and Westinghouse) or underwent dramatic transformation programs and internal reorganizations (GE and ABB). By the late 1980s, large multibusiness corporations were struggling to justify their existence. (See "What Ever Happened to the Dogs and Cash Cows?" at the end of this article.)

Not surprisingly, waves of new approaches to strategy were proposed to address these multiple assaults on the premises of strategic planning. Many focused inward. The lessons from Tom Peters and Bob Waterman's "excellent" companies led the way, closely followed by total quality management as strategy, reengineering, core competence, competing on capabilities, and the learning organization. Each approach made its contribution in turn, yet how any of them built on or refuted the previously accepted wisdom was unclear. The result: Each compounded the confusion about strategy that now besets managers.

A framework that has the potential to cut through much of this confusion is now emerging from the strategy field. The approach is grounded in economics, and it explains how a company's resources drive its performance in a dynamic competitive environment. Hence the umbrella term academics use to describe this work:

the *resource-based view of the firm* (RBV).[1] The RBV
combines the *internal* analysis of phenomena within
companies (a preoccupation of many management
gurus since the mid-1980s) with the *external* analysis of
the industry and the competitive environment (the
central focus of earlier strategy approaches). Thus the
resource-based view builds on, but does not replace,
the two previous broad approaches to strategy by
combining internal and external perspectives.[2] It
derives its strength from its ability to explain in clear
managerial terms why some competitors are more
profitable than others, how to put the idea of core
competence into practice, and how to develop diversification strategies that make sense. The resource-based
view, therefore, will be as powerful and as important to
strategy in the 1990s as industry analysis was in the
1980s. (See "A Brief History of Strategy" at the end of
this article.)

The RBV sees companies as very different collections
of physical and intangible assets and capabilities. No
two companies are alike because no two companies have
had the same set of experiences, acquired the same
assets and skills, or built the same organizational cultures. These assets and capabilities determine how efficiently and effectively a company performs its functional
activities. Following this logic, a company will be positioned to succeed if it has the best and most appropriate
stocks of resources for its business and strategy.

Valuable resources can take a variety of forms,
including some overlooked by the narrower conceptions
of core competence and capabilities. They can be *physical*, like the wire into your house. Potentially, both the
telephone and cable companies are in a very strong position to succeed in the brave new world of interactive

multimedia because they own the on-ramp to the information superhighway. Or valuable resources may be *intangible*, such as brand names or technological know-how. The Walt Disney Company, for example, holds a unique consumer franchise that makes Disney a success in a slew of businesses, from soft toys to theme parks to videos. Similarly, Sharp Corporation's knowledge of flat-panel display technology has enabled it to dominate the $7 billion worldwide liquid-crystal-display (LCD) business. Or the valuable resource may be an *organizational capability* embedded in a company's routines, processes, and culture. Take, for example, the skills of the Japanese automobile companies—first in low-cost, lean manufacturing; next in high-quality production; and then in fast product development. These capabilities, built up over time, transform otherwise pedestrian or commodity inputs into superior products and make the companies that have developed them successful in the global market.

Competitive advantage, whatever its source, ultimately can be attributed to the ownership of a valuable resource that enables the company to perform activities better or more cheaply than competitors. Marks & Spencer, for example, possesses a range of resources that demonstrably yield it a competitive advantage in British retailing. (See the exhibit "How Marks & Spencer's Resources Give It Competitive Advantage.") This is true both at the single-business level and at the corporate level, where the valuable resources might reside in a particular function, such as corporate research and development, or in an asset, such as corporate brand identity. Superior performance will therefore be based on developing a *competitively distinct* set of resources and deploying them in a well-conceived strategy.

Competitively Valuable Resources

Resources cannot be evaluated in isolation, because their value is determined in the interplay with market forces. A resource that is valuable in a particular industry or at a particular time might fail to have the same value in a different industry or chronological context. For example, despite several attempts to brand lobsters, so far no one has been successful in doing so. A brand name was once very important in the personal computer industry, but it no longer is, as IBM has discovered at great cost. Thus the RBV inextricably links a company's internal capabilities (what it does well) and its external

How Marks & Spencer's Resources Give It Competitive Advantage

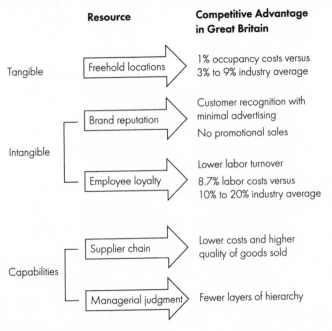

Resource	Competitive Advantage in Great Britain
Tangible	
Freehold locations	1% occupancy costs versus 3% to 9% industry average
Intangible	
Brand reputation	Customer recognition with minimal advertising / No promotional sales
Employee loyalty	Lower labor turnover / 8.7% labor costs versus 10% to 20% industry average
Capabilities	
Supplier chain	Lower costs and higher quality of goods sold
Managerial judgment	Fewer layers of hierarchy

industry environment (what the market demands and what competitors offer). Described that way, competing on resources sounds simple. In practice, however, managers often have a hard time identifying and evaluating their companies' resources objectively. The RBV can help by bringing discipline to the often fuzzy and subjective process of assessing valuable resources.

For a resource to qualify as the basis for an effective strategy, it must pass a number of external market tests of its value. (See the exhibit "What Makes a Resource Valuable?") Some are so straightforward that most managers grasp them intuitively or even unconsciously. For instance, a valuable resource must contribute to the production of something customers want at a price they are

What Makes a Resource Valuable?

Value creation zone

The dynamic interplay of three fundamental market forces determines the value of a resource or a capability.

willing to pay. Other tests are more subtle and, as a result, are commonly misunderstood or misapplied. These often turn out to cause strategies to misfire.

1. The test of inimitability: Is the resource hard to copy? Inimitability is at the heart of value creation because it limits competition. If a resource is inimitable, then any profit stream it generates is more likely to be sustainable. Possessing a resource that competitors easily can copy generates only temporary value. But because managers fail to apply this test rigorously, they try to base long-term strategies on resources that are imitable. IBP, the first meat-packing company in the United States to modernize, built a set of assets (automated plants located in cattle-rearing states) and capabilities (low-cost "disassembly" of beef) that enabled it to earn returns of 1.3% in the 1970s. By the late 1980s, however, ConAgra and Cargill had replicated these resources, and IBP's returns fell to 0.4%.

Inimitability doesn't last forever. Competitors eventually will find ways to copy most valuable resources. But managers can forestall them—and sustain profits for a while—by building their strategies around resources that have at least one of the following four characteristics:

The first is *physical uniqueness*, which almost by definition cannot be copied. A wonderful real estate location, mineral rights, or Merck & Company's pharmaceutical patents simply cannot be imitated. Although managers may be tempted to think that many of their resources fall into this category, on close inspection, few do.

A greater number of resources cannot be imitated because of what economists call *path dependency*. Simply put, these resources are unique and, therefore, scarce because of all that has happened along the path taken in their accumulation. As a result, competitors cannot go out and buy these resources instantaneously. Instead, they must be built over time in ways that are difficult to accelerate.[3]

The Gerber Products Company brand name for baby food, for example, is potentially imitable. Re-creating Gerber's brand loyalty, however, would take a very long time. Even if a competitor spent hundreds of millions of dollars promoting its baby food, it could not buy the trust that consumers associate with Gerber. That sort of brand connotation can be built only by marketing the product steadily for years, as Gerber has done. Similarly, crash R&D programs usually cannot replicate a successful technology when research findings cumulate. Having many researchers working in parallel cannot speed the process, because bottlenecks have to be solved sequentially. All this builds protection for the original resource.

The third source of inimitability is *causal ambiguity*. Would-be competitors are thwarted because it is impossible to disentangle either what the valuable resource is or how to re-create it. What *really* is the cause of Rubbermaid's continued success in plastic products? We can draw up lists of possible reasons. We can try, as any number of competitors have, to identify its recipe for innovation. But, in the final analysis, we cannot duplicate Rubbermaid's success.

Causally ambiguous resources are often organizational capabilities. These exist in a complex web of social interactions and may even depend critically on particular individuals. As Continental and United try to mimic Southwest's successful low-cost strategy, what will be most difficult for them to copy is not the planes, the routes, or the fast gate turnaround. All of those are readily observable and, in principle, easily duplicated. However, it will be difficult to reproduce Southwest's culture of fun, family, frugality, and focus because no one can quite specify exactly what it is or how it arose.

The final source of inimitability, *economic deterrence*, occurs when a company preempts a competitor by making a sizable investment in an asset. The competitor could replicate the resource but, because of limited market potential, chooses not to. This is most likely when strategies are built around large capital investments that are both scale sensitive and specific to a given market. For example, the minimum efficient scale for float-glass plants is so large that many markets can support only one such facility. Because such assets cannot be redeployed, they represent a credible commitment to stay and fight it out with competitors who try to replicate the investment. Faced with such a threat, potential imitators may choose not to duplicate the resource when the market is too small to support two players the size of the incumbent profitably. That is exactly what is now occurring in Eastern Europe. As companies rush to modernize, the first to build a float-glass facility in a country is likely to go unchallenged by competitors.

Banking on the durability of the most core competencies is risky. They have limited lives and will earn only temporary profits.

2. The test of durability: How quickly does this resource depreciate? The longer lasting a resource is, the more valuable it will be. Like inimitability, this test asks whether the resource can sustain competitive

advantage over time. While some industries are stable for years, managers today recognize that most are so dynamic that the value of resources depreciates quickly. Disney's brand name survived almost two decades of benign neglect between Walt Disney's death and the installation of Michael D. Eisner and his management team. In contrast, technological know-how in a fast-moving industry is a rapidly wasting asset, as the list of different companies that have dominated successive generations of semiconductor memories illustrates. Economist Joseph A. Schumpeter first recognized this phenomenon in the 1930s. He described waves of innovation that allow early movers to dominate the market and earn substantial profits. However, their valuable resources are soon imitated or surpassed by the next great innovation, and their superior profits turn out to be transitory. Schumpeter's description of major companies and whole industries blown away in a gale of "creative destruction" captures the

In practice, core competence has too often become a "feel good" exercise that no one fails.

pressure many managers feel today. Banking on the durability of most core competencies is risky. Most resources have a limited life and will earn only temporary profits.

3. The test of appropriability: Who captures the value that the resource creates? Not all profits from a resource automatically flow to the company that "owns" the resource. In fact, the value is always subject to bargaining among a host of players, including customers, distributors, suppliers, and employees. What has happened to leveraged buyout firms is revealing. A critical resource of LBO firms was the network of contacts and relationships in the investment banking community. However, this resource often resided in the individuals doing the deals, not in the LBO firms as a whole. These individuals could—and often did—depart to set up their own LBO funds or move to another firm where they could reap a greater share of the profits that their resource generated. Basing a strategy on resources that are not inextricably bound to the company can make profits hard to capture.

4. The test of substitutability: Can a unique resource be trumped by a different resource?

Since Michael E. Porter's introduction of the five-forces framework, every strategist has been on the lookout for the potential impact of substitute products. The steel industry, for example, has lost a major market in beer cans to aluminum makers in the past 20 years. The resource-based view pushes this critical question down a level to the resources that underpin a company's ability to deliver a good or service.

The greatest mistake managers make when evaluating their resources is failing to assess them relative to competitors'.

Consider the following example. In the early 1980s, People Express Airlines challenged the major airlines with a low-price strategy. Founder Donald C. Burr pursued this strategy by developing a unique no-frills approach and an infrastructure to deliver low-cost flights. Although the major airlines were unable to replicate this approach, they nevertheless were able to retaliate using a *different* resource to offer consumers equivalent low-cost fares—their computer reservation systems and yield-management skills. This substitution eventually drove People Express into bankruptcy and out of the industry.

5. The test of competitive superiority: Whose resource is really better? Perhaps the greatest mistake managers make when evaluating their companies' resources is that they do not assess them relative to competitors'. Core competence has too often become a "feel good" exercise that no one fails. Every company can identify one activity that it does relatively better than other activities and claim that as its core competence. Unfortunately, core competence should not be an internal assessment of which activity, of all its activities, the company performs best. It should be a harsh external assessment of what it does better than competitors, for which the term *distinctive competence* is more appropriate. How many consumer packaged-goods companies assert that their core competence is consumer marketing skills? They may indeed all be good at that activity, but a corporate strategy built on such a core competence will rapidly run into trouble because other competitors with better skills will be pursuing the same strategy.

The way to avoid the vacuousness of generic statements of core competence is to disaggregate the corporation's resources. The category *consumer marketing skills*, for example, is too broad. But it can be divided into subcategories such as effective brand management, which in turn can be divided into skills such as product-line extensions, cost-effective couponing, and so on. Only by looking at this level of specificity can we understand the sources of a company's uniqueness and measure by analyzing the data whether it is competitively superior on those dimensions. Can anyone evaluate whether Kraft General Foods' or Unilever's consumer marketing skills are better? No. But we can demonstrate quantitatively which is more successful at launching product-line extensions.

Disaggregation is important not only for identifying truly distinctive resources but also for deriving actionable implications. How many companies have developed a statement of their core competencies and then have struggled to know what to do with it? One manufacturer of medical-diagnostics test equipment, for example, defined one of its core competencies as instrumentation. But this intuitively obvious definition was too broad to be actionable. By pushing to deeper levels of disaggregation, the company came to a powerful insight. In fact, its strength in instrumentation was mainly attributable to its competitive superiority in designing the interface between its machines and the people who use them. As a result, the company decided to reinforce its valuable capability by hiring ergonomists, and it expanded into doctors' offices, a fast-growing segment of its market. There, the company's resources created a real competitive advantage, in part because its equipment can be operated by office personnel rather than only by technicians.

Although disaggregation is the key to identifying competitively superior resources, sometimes the valuable resource is a combination of skills, none of which is superior by itself but which, when combined, make a better package. Honeywell's industrial automation systems are successful in the marketplace—a measure that the company is good at something. Yet each individual component and software program might not be the best available. Competitive superiority lies either in the weighted average (the company does not rank first in any resource, but it is still better on average than any competitor) or in its system-integration capability.

The lesson for managers is that conclusions about critical resources should be based on objective data from the market. In our experience, managers often treat core competence as an exercise in intuition and skip the thorough research and detailed analysis needed to get the right answer.

Strategic Implications

Managers should build their strategies on resources that meet the five tests outlined above. The best of these resources are often intangible, not physical, hence the emphasis in recent approaches on the softer aspects of corporate assets—the culture, the technology, and the transformational leader. The tests capture how market forces determine the value of resources. They force managers to look inward and outward at the same time.

However, most companies are not ideally positioned with competitively valuable resources. More likely, they have a mixed bag of resources—some good, some mediocre, and some outright liabilities, such as IBM's monolithic mainframe culture. The harsh truth is that most companies' resources do not pass the objective application of the market tests.

Even those companies that are fortunate enough to have unusual assets or capabilities are not home free. Valuable resources must still be joined with other resources and embedded in a set of functional policies and activities that distinguish the company's position in the market—after all, competitors can have core competencies, too.

Strategy requires managers to look forward as well. Companies fortunate enough to have a truly distinctive competence must also be wise enough to realize that its value is eroded by time and competition. Consider what happened to Xerox. During what has become known as its "lost decade," the 1970s, Xerox believed its reprographic capability to be inimitable. And while Xerox slept, Canon took over world leadership in photocopiers.

In a world of continuous change, companies need to maintain pressure constantly at the frontiers—building for the next round of competition. Managers must therefore continually invest in and upgrade their resources, however good those resources are today, and leverage them with effective strategies into attractive industries in which they can contribute to a competitive advantage.

INVESTING IN RESOURCES

Because all resources depreciate, an effective corporate strategy requires continual investment in order to maintain and build valuable resources. One of Eisner's first actions as CEO at Disney was to revive the company's commitment to animation. He invested $50 million in *Who Framed Roger Rabbit?* to create the company's first animated feature-film hit in many years and quadrupled its output of animated feature films—bringing out successive hits, such as *Beauty and the Beast, Aladdin,* and *The Lion King.*

Similarly, Marks & Spencer has periodically reexamined its position in its only business—retailing—and has made major investments to stay competitive. In the early 1980s, the British company spent billions on store renovation, opened new edge-of-town locations, and updated its procurement and distribution systems. In contrast, the U.S. retailer Sears, Roebuck and Company diversified into insurance, real estate, and stock brokerages, while failing to keep up with the shift in retailing to new mall locations and specialty stores.

The mandate to reinvest in strategic resources may seem obvious. The great contribution of the core competence notion is its recognition that, in corporations with a traditional divisional structure, investment in the corporation's resources often takes a backseat to optimizing current divisional profitability. Core competence, therefore, identifies the critical role that the corporate office has to play as the guardian of what are, in essence, the crown jewels of the corporation. In some instances, such guardianship might even require explicitly establishing a corporate officer in charge of nurturing the critical resources. Cooper Industries, a diversified manufacturer, established a manufacturing services group to disseminate the best manufacturing practices throughout the company. The group helped "Cooperize" acquired companies, rationalizing and improving their production facilities. The head of the services group, Joseph R. Coppola, was of a caliber to be hired away as CEO of Giddings & Lewis, the largest U.S. machine tool manufacturer. Similarly, many professional service firms, such as Coopers & Lybrand, have a senior partner in charge of their critical capabilities—client-relationship management, staff training, and intellectual development. Valuable corporate resources are often supradivisional, and, unless someone is managing them on that basis, divisions will underinvest in them or free ride on them.

At the same time, investing in core competencies without examining the competitive dynamics that deter-

mine industry attractiveness is dangerous. By ignoring
the marketplace, managers risk investing heavily in
resources that will yield low returns. Masco Corporation
did exactly that. It built a competence in metalworking
and diversified into tightly related industries. Unfortunately, the returns from this strategy were lower than
the company had expected. Why? A straightforward
five-forces analysis would have revealed that the structure of the industries Masco entered was poor—buyers
were price sensitive with limited switching costs, entry
barriers were low, and suppliers were powerful. Despite
Masco's metalworking expertise, its industry context
prevented it from achieving exceptional returns until it
developed the skills that enabled it to enter more attractive industries.

Similarly, if competitors are ignored, the profits that
could result from a successful resource-based strategy
will dissipate in the struggle to acquire those resources.
Consider the value of the cable wire into your house as a
source of competitive advantage in the multimedia
industry. Companies such as Time Warner have been
forced by competitors, who can also see the value of that
wire, to bid billions of dollars to acquire control of even
modest cable systems. As a result, they may never realize
substantial returns on their investment. This is true not
only for resources acquired on the market but also for
those core competencies that many competitors are
simultaneously trying to develop internally.

UPGRADING RESOURCES

What if a company has no unusually valuable resources?
Unfortunately, that is a common experience when
resources are evaluated against the standard of competitive superiority. Or what if a company's valuable

resources have been imitated or substituted by competitors? Or perhaps its resources, like Masco's, are valuable only in industries so structurally unattractive that, regardless of how efficiently it operates, its financial returns will never be stellar. In these cases—indeed, in nearly all cases—companies must continually upgrade the number and quality of their resources and associated competitive positions in order to hold off the almost inevitable decay in their value.

Upgrading resources means moving beyond what the company is already good at, which can be accomplished in a number of ways. The first is by adding new resources, the way Intel Corporation added a brand name, Intel Inside, to its technological resource base. The second is by upgrading to alternative resources that are threatening the company's current capabilities. AT&T is trying to build capabilities in multimedia now that its physical infrastructure—the network—is no longer unique or as critical as it once was. Finally, a company can upgrade its resources in order to move into a structurally more attractive industry, the way Nucor Corporation, a U.S. steel company, has made the transition from competitive, low-margin, down-stream businesses, such as steel joists, into more differentiated, upstream businesses, such as thin-slab cast-steel sheets.

Ironically, many diversification efforts fail because even the companies that own valuable resources can't replicate them.

Perhaps the most successful examples of upgrading resources are in companies that have added new competencies sequentially, often over extended periods of time. Sharp provides a wonderful illustration of how to exploit a virtuous circle of sequentially upgrading technologies and products, what the Japanese call "seeds and needs."

In the late 1950s, Sharp was an assembler of televisions and radios, seemingly condemned to the second rank of Japanese consumer electronics companies. To break out of that position, founder Tokuji Hayakawa, who had always stressed the importance of innovation, created a corporate R&D facility. When the Japanese Ministry of International Trade and Industry blocked Sharp from designing computers, the company used its limited technology to produce the world's first digital calculator in 1964. To strengthen its position in this business, Sharp backward integrated into manufacturing its own specialized semiconductors and made a strong commitment to the new liquid-crystal-display technology. Sharp's bet on LCD technology paid off and enabled it to develop a number of new products, such as the Wizard electronic organizer. Over time, the superiority of its display technology gave Sharp a competitive advantage in businesses it had previously struggled in, such as camcorders. Its breakthrough product, Viewcam, captured 20% of the Japanese market within six months of release in 1992.

At each stage, Sharp took on a new challenge, whether to develop or improve a technology or to enter or attack a market. Success in each endeavor improved the company's resources in technology, distribution, and organizational capability. It also opened new avenues for expansion. Today, Sharp is the dominant player in the LCD market and a force in consumer electronics.

Cooper provides another example. Challenged to justify its plan to acquire Champion Spark Plug Company in 1989, when fuel injection was replacing spark plugs, Cooper reasoned that it had the resources to help Champion improve its position, as it had done many times before with products such as Crescent wrenches, Nicholson files, and Gardner-Denver mining equipment. But what really swung the decision, according to Cooper chairman and CEO Robert Cizik, was the recognition that Cooper lacked a critical skill it needed for the future—the ability to manage international manufacturing. With its numerous overseas plants, Champion offered Cooper the opportunity to acquire global management capabilities. The Champion acquisition, in Cizik's view, was a way to upgrade Cooper's resources. Indeed, a review of the company's history shows that Cooper has deliberately sought to improve its capabilities gradually by periodically taking on challenges it knows will have a high degree of difficulty for the organization.

LEVERAGING RESOURCES

Corporate strategies must strive to leverage resources into all the markets in which those resources contribute to competitive advantage or to compete in new markets that improve the corporate resources. Or, preferably, both, as with Cooper's acquisition of Champion. Failure to do so, as occurred with Disney following the death of its founder, leads a company to be under-valued. Eisner's management team, which extended the scope of Disney's activities into hotels, retailing, and publishing, was installed in response to a hostile-takeover threat triggered by the under-utilization of the company's valuable resources.

Good corporate strategy, then, requires continual reassessment of the company's scope. The question strategists must ask is, How far can the company's valuable resource be extended across markets? The answer will vary widely because resources differ greatly in their specificity, from highly fungible resources (such as cash, many kinds of machinery, and general management skills) to much more specialized resources (such as expertise in narrow scientific disciplines and secret product formulas). Specialized resources often play a critical role in securing competitive advantage, but, because they are so specific, they lose value quickly when they are moved away from their original settings. Shell Oil Company's brand name, for example, will not transfer well outside autos and energy, however valuable it is within those fields. Highly fungible resources, on the other hand, transfer well across a wide range of markets but rarely constitute the key source of competitive advantage.

The RBV helps us understand why the track record of corporate diversification has been so poor and identifies three common and costly strategic errors companies make when they try to grow by leveraging resources. First, managers tend to over-estimate the transferability of specific assets and capabilities. The irony is that because valuable resources are hard to imitate, the company itself may find it difficult to replicate them in new markets. Despite its great success in Great Britain, Marks & Spencer has failed repeatedly in attempts to leverage its resources in the North American market—a classic example of misjudging the important role that context plays in competitive advantage. In this case, the concepts of path dependency and causal ambiguity are both at work. Marks & Spencer's success is rooted in its 100-year reputation for excellence in Great Britain and in the skills and relationships that enable it to manage its domestic supply chain effectively. Just as British competitors have been unable to duplicate this set of advantages, Marks & Spencer itself struggles to do so when it tries to enter a new market against established competitors.

Second, managers overestimate their ability to compete in highly profitable industries. Such industries are often attractive precisely because entry barriers limit the number of competitors. Entry barriers are really resource barriers: The reason competitors find it so hard to enter the business is that accumulating the necessary resources is difficult. If it could be done easily, competitors would flock to the opportunity, driving down average returns. Many managers fail to see the connection between company-level resources and industry-level profits and convince themselves that they can vault the entry barrier, without considering which factors will ultimately determine success in the industry. Philip Morris Companies' entry into soft drinks, for example, foundered on the difficulties it faced managing the franchise distribution network. After years of poor performance in that business, it gave up and divested 7-Up.

The third common diversification mistake is to assume that leveraging generic resources, such as lean manufacturing, will be a major source of competitive advantage in a new market—regardless of the specific competitive dynamics of that market. Chrysler Corporation seems to have learned this lesson.

Newell's success comes from deploying its capabilities in a structurally attractive industry.

Expecting that its skills in design and manufacturing would ensure success in the aerospace industry, Chrysler acquired Gulfstream Aerospace Corporation—only to divest it five years later in order to concentrate on its core businesses.

Despite the common pitfalls, the rewards for companies that leverage their resources appropriately, as Disney has, are high. Newell Company is another stunning example of a company that has built a set of capabilities and used them to secure commanding positions for products in a wide range of industries. Newell was a modest manufacturer of drapery hardware in 1967, when a new CEO, Daniel C. Ferguson, articulated its strategy: The company would specialize in high-volume production of a variety of household and office staple goods that would be sold through mass merchandisers. The company made a series of acquisitions, each of which benefited from Newell's capabilities—its focused control systems; its computer links with mass discounters, which facilitate paperless invoicing and automatic inventory restocking; and its expertise in the "good-better-best" merchandising of basic products, in which retailers typically choose to carry only one brand, with several quality and price levels. In turn, each acquisition gave Newell yet another opportunity to strengthen its capabilities. Today, Newell holds leading market positions in drapery hardware, cookware, glassware, paintbrushes, and office products and maintains an impressive 15% earnings growth annually. What differentiates this diversified company from a host of others is how it has been able to use its corporate resources to establish and maintain competitive advantage at the business-unit level.

However, even Newell benefits from the attractiveness of the markets in which it competes. All its products are infrequently purchased, low-cost items. Most consumers will not spend time comparison shopping for six glasses, nor do they have a sense of the market price. Do you know if $3.99 is too much to pay for a brass curtain rod? Thus Newell's resources are all the more valuable for being deployed in an attractive industry context.

W<small>HETHER A COMPANY</small> is building a strategy based on core competencies, is developing a learning organization, or is in the middle of a transformation process, those concepts can all be interpreted as a mandate to build a unique set of resources and capabilities. However, this must be done with a sharp eye on the dynamic industry context and competitive situation, rigorously applying market tests to those resources. Strategy that blends two powerful sets of insights about capabilities and competition represents an enduring logic that transcends management fads.

That this approach pays off is demonstrated by the impressive performance of companies such as Newell, Cooper, Disney, and Sharp. Although these companies may not have set out explicitly to craft resource-based strategies, they nonetheless capture the power of this logic and the returns that come to those who do.

What Ever Happened to the Dogs and Cash Cows?

IN THE LATE 1960s and early 1970s, the wisdom of the day was that companies could transfer the competitive advantage of professional management across a broad range of businesses. Many companies responded to the perceived opportunity: Armed with decentralized structures and limited, but tight, financial controls, they diversified into a number of related and unrelated businesses, mostly through acquisition. In time, such conglomerates came to resemble miniature economies in their own right.

There appeared to be no compelling limits to the scope of corporations.

As the first oil crisis hit in 1973, corporate managers faced deteriorating performance and had little advice on how to act. Into this vacuum came the Boston Consulting Group and portfolio management. In BCG's now famous growth/share matrix, corporate management was finally given a tool with which to reassert control over its many divisions.

This simple matrix allowed managers to classify each division, since renamed a strategic business unit, into a quadrant based on the growth of its industry, and the relative strength of the unit's competitive position. There was a prescribed strategy for each position in the matrix: sustain the cash-generating cows, divest or harvest the dogs, take cash from the cows and invest in question marks in order to make them stars, and increase the market share of the stars until their industry growth slowed and they became the next generation of cash cows. Such simple prescriptions gave corporate management both a sense of what their strategy should accomplish—a balanced portfolio of businesses—and a way to control and allocate resources to their divisions.

The problem with the portfolio matrix was that it did not address how value was being created across the divisions, which could be as diverse as semiconductors and hammers. The only relationship between them was cash. As we have come to learn, the relatedness of businesses is at the heart of value creation in diversified companies. The portfolio matrix also suffered from its assumption that corporations had to be self-sufficient in capital. That implied that they should find a use for all internally generated cash and that they could not raise additional funds from the capital market. The capital markets of the 1980s demonstrated the fallacy of such assumptions.

In addition, the growth/share matrix failed to compare the competitive advantage a business received from being owned by a particular company with the costs of owning it. In the 1980s, many companies built enormous corporate infrastructures that created only small gains at the business-unit level. During the same period, the market for corporate control heated up, focusing attention on value for shareholders. Many companies with supposedly model portfolios were accordingly dissolved.

A Brief History of Strategy

THE FIELD OF STRATEGY has largely been shaped around a framework first conceived by Kenneth R. Andrews in his classic book *The Concept of Corporate Strategy* (Richard D. Irwin, 1971). Andrews defined strategy as the match between what a company *can* do (organizational strengths and weaknesses) within the universe of what it *might* do (environmental opportunities and threats).

Although the power of Andrews's framework was recognized from the start, managers were given few insights about how to assess either side of the equation systematically. The first important breakthrough came in Michael E. Porter's book *Competitive Strategy: Techniques for Analyzing Industries and Competitors* (Free Press, 1980). Porter's work built on the structure-conduct-performance paradigm of industrial-organization economics. The essence of the model is that the structure of an industry determines the state of competition within that industry and sets the context for companies' conduct—that is, their strategy. Most important, structural forces (which Porter called the five forces) determine the average profitability of the industry and have a correspondingly strong impact on the profitability of individual corporate strategies.

This analysis put the spotlight on choosing the "right industries" and, within them, the most attractive competitive positions. Although the model did not ignore the characteristics of individual companies, the emphasis was clearly on phenomena at the industry level.

With the appearance of the concepts of core competence and competing on capabilities, the pendulum swung dramatically in the other direction, moving from outside to inside the company. These approaches emphasized the importance both of the skills and collective learning embedded in an organization and of management's ability to marshal them. This view assumed that the roots of competitive advantage were inside the organization and that the adoption of new strategies was constrained by the current level of the company's resources. The external environment received little, if any, attention, and what we had learned about industries and competitive analysis seemed to disappear from our collective psyche. The emerging resource-based view of the firm helps to bridge these seemingly disparate approaches and to fulfill the promise of Andrews's framework. Like the capabilities approaches, the resource-based view acknowledges the importance of company-specific resources and competencies, yet it does so in the context of the competitive environment. The resource-based view shares another important characteristic with industry analysis: It, too, relies on economic reasoning. It sees capabilities and resources as the heart of a company's competitive position, subject to the interplay of three fundamental market forces: demand (does it meet customers' needs, and is it competitively superior?), scarcity (is it imitable or substitutable, and is it durable?), and appropriability (who owns the profits?). The five tests described in the article translate these general economic requirements into specific, actionable terms.

Notes

1. A number of insightful articles have been written on the resource-based view, including: Birger Wernerfelt, "A Resource-Based View of the Firm," *Strategic Management Journal*, September–October 1984, p. 171; J.B. Barney, "Strategic Factor Markets: Expectations, Luck and Business Strategy," *Management Science*, October 1986, p. 1,231; Richard P. Rumelt, "Theory, Strategy, and Entrepreneurship," in *The Competitive Challenge: Strategies for Industrial Innovation and Renewal*, ed. David J. Teece (Cambridge, Mass.: Ballinger, 1987), p. 137; Ingemar Dierickx and Karel Cool, "Asset Stock Accumulation and Sustainability of Competitive Advantage," *Management Science*, December 1989, p. 1,504; Kathleen R. Conner, "A Historical Comparison of Resource-Based Theory and Five Schools of Thought Within Industrial Organization Economics: Do We Have a New Theory of the Firm?" *Journal of Management*, March 1991, p. 121; Raphael Amit and Paul J.H. Schoemaker, "Strategic Assets and Organizational Rent," *Strategic Management Journal*, January 1993, p. 33; and Margaret A. Peteraf, "The Cornerstones of Competitive Advantage: A Resource-Based View," *Strategic Management Journal*, March 1993, p. 179.

2. To date, the most attention paid to the integration of the two perspectives has been by Michael E. Porter in

Competitive Advantage: Creating and Sustaining Superior Performance (New York: Free Press, 1985) and, in the dynamic context, in his article "Towards a Dynamic Theory of Strategy," *Strategic Management Journal*, Winter 1991, p. 95.

3. These ideas were first discussed in two articles published in *Management Science*: Ingemar Dierickx and Karel Cool, "Asset Stock Accumulation and Sustainability of Competitive Advantage," December 1989, p. 1,504; and J.B. Barney, "Asset Stocks and Sustained Competitive Advantage," December 1989, p. 1,512.

Originally published in July–August 1995
Reprint 95403

Desperately Seeking Synergy

MICHAEL GOOLD AND

ANDREW CAMPBELL

Executive Summary

CORPORATE EXECUTIVES HAVE STRONG BIASES in
favor of synergy, and those biases can lead them into ill-
advised attempts to force business units to cooperate—
even when the ultimate benefits are unclear. But executives *can* separate the real opportunities from the
mirages, say Michael Goold and Andrew Campbell.
They simply need to take a more disciplined approach
to synergy.

These biases take four forms. First comes the *synergy
bias*, which leads executives to overestimate the benefits
and underestimate the costs of synergy. Then comes the
parenting bias, a belief that synergy will be captured
only by cajoling or compelling business units to cooperate. The parenting bias is usually accompanied by the
skills bias—the assumption that whatever know-how is
required to achieve synergy will be available within the

63

organization. Finally, executives fall victim to the *upside bias*, which causes them to concentrate so hard on the potential benefits of synergy that they overlook the possible downside risks.

In combination, these four biases make synergy seem more attractive and more easily achievable than it truly is. As a result, corporate executives often launch initiatives that ultimately waste time and money and sometimes even severely damage their businesses.

To avoid such failures, executives need to subject all synergy opportunities to a clear-eyed analysis that clarifies the benefits to be gained, examines the potential for corporate involvement, and takes into account the possible downsides. Such a disciplined approach will inevitably mean that fewer initiatives will be launched. But those that are pursued will be far more likely to deliver substantial gains.

THE PURSUIT OF SYNERGY PERVADES the management of most large companies. Meetings and retreats are held to brainstorm about ways to collaborate more effectively. Cross-business teams are set up to develop key account plans, coordinate product development, and disseminate best practices. Incentives for sharing knowledge, leads, and customers are built into complex compensation schemes. Processes and procedures are standardized. Organizational structures are reshuffled to accommodate new, cross-unit managerial positions.

The pursuit of synergy often distracts managers' attention from the nuts and bolts of business.

What emerges from all this activity? In our years of research into corporate synergy, we have found that synergy initiatives often fall short of management's expectations. Some never get beyond a few perfunctory meetings. Others generate a quick burst of activity and then slowly peter out. Others become permanent corporate fixtures without ever fulfilling their original goals. If the only drawbacks to such efforts were frustration and embarrassment, they might be viewed benignly as "learning experiences." But the pursuit of synergy often represents a major opportunity cost as well. It distracts managers' attention from the nuts and bolts of their businesses, and it crowds out other initiatives that might generate real benefits. Sometimes, the synergy programs actually backfire, eroding customer relationships, damaging brands, or undermining employee morale. Simply put, many synergy efforts end up destroying value rather than creating it.

Avoiding such failures is possible, but it requires a whole new way of looking at and thinking about synergy. Rather than assuming that synergy exists, can be achieved, and will be beneficial, corporate executives need to take a more balanced, even skeptical view. They need to counter synergy's natural allure by subjecting their instincts to rigorous evaluation. Such an approach will help executives avoid wasting precious resources on synergy programs that are unlikely to succeed. Perhaps even more important, it will enable them to better understand where the true synergy opportunities lie in their organizations. (See "What Is Synergy?" at the end of this article.)

We believe that synergy can provide a big boost to the bottom line of most large companies. The challenge is to separate the real opportunities from the illusions.

With a more disciplined approach, executives can realize greater value from synergy—even while pursuing fewer initiatives.

Four Managerial Biases

When a synergy program founders, it is usually the business units that take the blame. Corporate executives chalk the failure up to line managers' recalcitrance or incompetence. We have found, however, that the blame is frequently misplaced. The true cause more often lies in the thinking of the corporate executives themselves.

Because executives view the achievement of synergy as central to their jobs, they are prone to four biases that distort their thinking. First comes the *synergy bias*, which leads them to overestimate the benefits and underestimate the costs of synergy. Then comes the *parenting bias*, a belief that synergy will only be captured by cajoling or compelling the business units to cooperate. The parenting bias is usually accompanied by the *skills bias*—the assumption that whatever know-how is required to achieve synergy will be available within the organization. Finally, executives fall victim to the *upside bias*, which causes them to concentrate so hard on the potential benefits of synergy that they overlook the downsides. In combination, these four biases make synergy seem more attractive and more easily achievable than it truly is.

SYNERGY BIAS

Most corporate executives, whether or not they have any special insight into synergy opportunities or aptitude for nurturing collaboration, feel they *ought* to be creating

synergy. The achievement of synergy among their businesses is inextricably linked to their sense of their work
and their worth. In part, the synergy bias reflects executives' need to justify the existence of their corporation,
particularly to investors. "If we can't find opportunities
for synergy, there's no point to the group," one chief
executive explained to us. In part, it reflects their desire
to make the different businesses feel that they are part
of a single family. "My job is to create a family—a group
of managers who see themselves as members of one
team," commented another CEO. Perhaps most fundamentally, it reflects executives' real fear that they would
be left without a role if they were not able to promote
coordination, standardization, and other links among
the various businesses they control.

The synergy bias becomes an obsession for some
executives. Desperately seeking synergy, they make
unwise decisions and investments. In one international
food company that we studied—we'll call it Worldwide
Foods—a newly appointed chief executive fell victim to
such an obsession. Seeing that the company's various
national units operated autonomously, sharing few ideas
across borders, he became convinced that the key to
higher corporate profits—and a higher stock price—
lay in greater interunit cooperation. The creation of
synergy became his top priority, and he quickly
appointed global category managers to coordinate each
of Worldwide Foods' main product lines. Their brief was
to promote collaboration and standardization across
countries in order to "leverage the company's brands
internationally."

Pressured by the CEO, the category managers
launched a succession of high-profile synergy initiatives.
The results were dismal. A leading U.K. cookie brand

was launched with considerable expense in the United States. It promptly flopped. A pasta promotion that had worked well in Germany was rolled out in Italy and Spain. It backfired, eroding both margins and market shares. An attempt was made to standardize ingredients across Europe for some confectionery products in order to achieve economies of scale in purchasing and manufacturing. Consumers balked at buying the reformulated products.

Rather than encouraging interunit cooperation, the initiatives ended up discouraging it. As the failures mounted, the management teams in each country became more convinced than ever that their local markets were unique, requiring different products and marketing programs. After a year of largely fruitless efforts, with few tangible benefits and a significant deterioration in the relationship between the corporate center and the units, the chief executive began to retreat, curtailing the synergy initiatives.

A similar problem arose in a professional services firm. Created through a series of acquisitions, this firm had three consulting practices—organization development, employee benefits, and corporate strategy—as well as an executive search business. The chief executive believed that in order to justify the acquisitions, he needed to impose a "one-firm" policy on the four units. The centerpiece of this policy was the adoption of a coordinated approach to key accounts. A client-service manager was assigned to each major client and given responsibility for managing the overall relationship and for cross-selling the firm's various services.

The approach proved disastrous. The chief executive's enthusiasm for the one-firm policy blinded him to the realities of the marketplace. Most of the big clients resented the imposition of a gatekeeper between themselves and the actual providers of the specialist services they were buying. Indeed, many of them began to turn to the firm's competitors. Far from creating value, the synergy effort damaged the firm's profitability, not to mention some of its most important client relationships. Faced with an uproar from the consulting staff, the CEO was forced to eliminate the client-manager positions.

For both these chief executives, synergy had become an emotional imperative rather than a rational one. Spurred by a desire to find and express the logic that held their portfolio of businesses together, they simply assumed that synergies did exist and could be achieved. Like wanderers in a desert who see oases where there is only sand, they became so entranced by the idea of synergy that they led their companies to pursue mirages.

PARENTING BIAS

Corporate managers afflicted with the synergy bias are prone to other biases as well. If they believe that opportunities for synergy exist, they feel compelled to get involved themselves. They assume that the unit managers, overly focused on their own businesses and overly protective of their own authority, disregard or undervalue opportunities to collaborate with one another. As one exasperated CEO told us, "There's the I'm-too-busy syndrome, the not-invented-here syndrome, and the don't-interfere-you-don't-understand-my-business syndrome. If I didn't continually bang their

If business-unit managers choose not to cooperate in a synergy initiative, they usually have good reasons.

heads together, I believe they would never talk to one another."

Assuming that unit managers are naturally resistant to cooperation, executives conclude that synergy can be achieved only through the intervention of the parent. (The parent, in our terminology, can be a holding company, a corporate center, a division, or any other body that oversees more than one business unit.) In most cases, however, both the assumption and the conclusion are wrong. Business managers have every reason to forge links with other units when those links will make their own business more successful. After all, they regularly team up with outside organizations—suppliers, customers, or joint venture partners—and they'll even cooperate with direct competitors if it's in their interest. In the music industry, to take just one example, the four leading companies will often share the same CD-manufacturing plant in countries with insufficient sales to support four separate plants.

If business-unit managers choose not to cooperate, they usually have good reasons. Either they don't believe there are any benefits to be gained or they believe the costs, including the opportunity costs, outweigh the benefits. The fact that unit managers do not always share their bosses' enthusiasm for a proposed linkage is not evidence that they suffer from the not-invented-here syndrome or some other attitudinal ailment. It may simply be they've concluded that no real gains will come of the effort.

At Worldwide Foods, for example, one of the corporate category managers attempted to create an advertising campaign that could be used throughout Europe. The single campaign seemed logical: It would promote a unified brand and would be cheaper to produce than a series of country-specific campaigns. And, because the campaign would be funded at the corporate level, the category manager presumed it would be attractive to the local managers, who would not have to dip into their own budgets. But several local managers resoundingly rejected the corporate advertisements, in many cases choosing to produce their own ads with their own money. The category manager, regarding the rejection as evidence of local-manager intransigence, asked the chief executive to impose the corporate advertising as a matter of policy. "How parochial can you get?" he complained. "They're even willing to pay out good money for their own ads rather than go along with the ones produced by my department."

But discussions with the local managers revealed that their rejection of the corporate campaign was neither reactionary nor irrational. They believed that the corporate campaign ignored real differences in local markets, cultures, and customs. The pan-European advertising campaign would simply not have worked in countries such as Germany, Sweden, and Denmark.

Believing unit managers to be naturally resistant to cooperation, parent executives often feel compelled to intervene.

"I'd have been delighted to get my advertising for free from corporate," stated the German product manager. "But I'd have paid much more heavily in terms of lost market share if I'd used their campaign. We had to go our own way because the corporate campaign wasn't appropriate for our distribution channels or target customers."

Because the parenting bias encourages corporate executives to discount unit managers' objections, it often leads them to interfere excessively, doing more harm than good. If, for example, unit managers believe that the opportunity costs of a synergy program outweigh its benefits, forcing them to cooperate will make them even more skeptical of synergy. If two unit managers have a bad working relationship, pushing ahead with a coordination committee will simply waste everyone's time. Although headquarters sometimes needs to push units to cooperate—when, for instance, some units are unaware of promising technical or operational innovations in another unit—it should consider intervention a last resort, not a first priority.

SKILLS BIAS

Corporate executives who believe they should intervene are also likely to assume that they have the skills to intervene effectively. All too often, however, they don't. The members of the management team may lack the operating knowledge, personal relationships, or facilitative skills required to achieve meaningful collaboration, or they may simply lack the patience and force of character needed to follow through. In combination with the parenting bias, the skills bias dooms many synergy programs.

In one large retailing group, the chief executive was convinced, rightly, that there were big benefits to be had from improving and sharing logistics skills across the company. Knowing that competitors were gaining advantages from faster, cheaper distribution, he felt, again rightly, that his businesses were not giving this function sufficient attention. He therefore set up a cross-business team to develop, as he put it, "a core corporate competence in logistics." As there was no obvious corporate candidate to lead the team, the chief executive decided to appoint the supply chain manager from the company's biggest business unit, in the belief that he would grow into the role. As it turned out, the manager's lack of state-of-the-art logistics know-how, combined with his poor communication skills, undermined the team's efforts. The whole initiative quickly fell apart.

The skills bias is a natural corollary to the parenting bias. If you are convinced that you need to intervene to make synergies happen, you are likely to overlook skills gaps—or at least assume that they can be filled when necessary. Professional pride, moreover, can make it difficult for senior managers to recognize that they and their colleagues lack certain capabilities. But a lack of the right skills can fatally undermine the implementation of any synergy initiative, however big the opportunity. What's more, learning new skills is not easy, especially for senior managers with ingrained ways of doing things. If new and unfamiliar skills are called for, it's a serious error to underestimate the difficulty of building them. It may be better to pass the opportunity by than to embark on an intervention that can't be successfully implemented.

UPSIDE BIAS

Whether or not the intended benefits of a synergy initiative materialize, the initiative can have other, often unforeseen consequences—what we call *knock-on effects*. Knock-on effects can be either beneficial or harmful, and they can take many forms. A corporate-led synergy program may, for example, help or harm an effort to instill employees with greater personal accountability for business performance. It may reinforce or impede an organizational change. It may increase or reduce employee motivation and innovation. Or it may alter the way unit managers think about their businesses and their roles, for better or for worse.

In evaluating the potential for synergy, corporate executives tend to focus too much on positive knock-on effects while overlooking the downsides. In large part, this upside bias is a natural accompaniment to the synergy bias: if parent managers are inclined to think the best of synergy, they will look for evidence that backs up their position while avoiding evidence to the contrary. The upside bias is also reinforced by the general belief that cooperation, sharing, and teamwork are intrinsically good for organizations.

In fact, collaboration is not always good for organizations. Sometimes, it's downright bad. In one consulting company, for example, two business units decided to form a joint team to market and deliver a new service for a client. One of the business units did information technology consulting, the other did strategy consulting. One evening, when the team was working late, the strategy consultants suggested that they order in some pizza and charge it to the client. The IT consultants were surprised, since their terms of employment did not allow them to charge such items to client accounts. The conversation then turned to terms and conditions more generally, and soon the IT consultants discovered that the strategy consultants were being paid as much as 50% more and had better fringe benefits. Yet here they were working together doing similar kinds of tasks.

> *The downsides of synergy are every bit as real as the upsides; they are just not seen as clearly.*

The discovery of the different billing and compensation practices—what became known in the firm as the
"pizza problem"—caused dissatisfaction among the IT
consultants and friction between the two businesses. An
attempt to resolve the problem by moving some IT consultants into the strategy business only made matters
worse. Few of the IT consultants achieved high ratings
under the strategy unit's evaluation criteria; consequently,
many of the firm's best IT consultants ended up quitting.

As the pizza problem shows, viewing cooperation as
an unalloyed good often blinds corporate executives to
the negative knock-on effects that may arise from synergy programs. They rush to promote cooperative efforts
as examples to be emulated throughout the company.
Rarely, though, do they kill an otherwise promising initiative for fear that it might erode a unit's morale or distort its culture. Synergy's downsides are every bit as real
as its upsides; they're just not seen as clearly.

The best antidotes for these four biases, as for all
biases, are awareness and discipline. Simply by acknowl-
edging the tendency to overstate the benefits and feasibility of synergy, executives can better spot distortions
in their thinking. They can then put their ideas to the
test, posing hard questions to themselves and to their
colleagues: What exactly are we trying to achieve, and
how big is the benefit? Is there anything to be gained by
intervening at the corporate level? What are the possible
downsides? The answers to these questions tell them
whether and how to act.

Sizing the Prize

The goals of synergy programs tend to be expressed in
broad, vague terms: "sharing best practices," "coordinat-

ing customer relationships," "cross-fertilizing ideas." In addition to cutting off debate—who, after all, wants to argue against sharing?—such fuzzy language obscures rather than clarifies the real costs and benefits of the programs. It also tends to undermine implementation, leading to scattershot, unfocused efforts as different parties impose their own views about what needs to be done to reach the imprecisely stated goals.

Clarifying the objectives and benefits of a potential synergy initiative is the first and most important discipline in making sound decisions on synergy.

Clarifying the real objectives and benefits of a potential synergy initiative—"sizing the prize," as we term it—is the first and most important discipline in making sound decisions on synergy. Executives should strive to be as precise as possible about both the type of synergy being sought and its ultimate payoff for the company. Overarching goals should be disaggregated into discrete, well-defined benefits, and then each benefit should be subjected to hard-nosed financial analysis.

At Worldwide Foods, for example, one of the newly appointed category managers found that her initial efforts were being frustrated by the imprecision of the CEO's goal. "Leveraging international brands" covered such a wide range of possible objectives, from standardizing brand positioning, to sharing marketing programs, to coordinating product rollouts, that she found it difficult to reach agreement about tasks and priorities with the various local managers.

During a visit to the company's Argentinean subsidiary, for example, she tried to persuade the local product manager to use a marketing campaign that had been successful in other countries. Dismissing the idea, he tried to shift the discussion. "That campaign wouldn't work in Argentina," he said. "What I would like is advice on new-product-development processes."

"I don't think you understand," the category manager countered. "I'm trying to create an international brand, and that means standardizing marketing across countries."

"No," said the local manager. "If we want to leverage our brands, we need to focus on product development."

Everywhere she went, the category manager found herself mired in similarly fruitless debates. All the local managers defined "leveraging international brands" to mean what they wanted it to mean. There was no common ground on which to build.

Finally, the category manager stepped back and tried to think more clearly about the synergy opportunities. She saw that the broad goal—leveraging international brands—could be broken down into three separate components: making the brand recognizable across borders, reducing duplicated effort, and increasing the flow of marketing know-how. Each of these components could, in turn, be disaggregated further. Making the brand recognizable, for instance, might involve a number of different efforts affecting such areas as brand positioning, pricing, packaging, ingredients, and advertising. Each of these efforts could then be evaluated separately on its own merits. (See the exhibit "Disaggregating a Synergy Program.")

The exercise proved extremely useful. The category manager was able to go back to the local managers and systematically discuss each possible synergy effort, identifying in precise terms its ramifications for each local unit. In some cases, she found she had to take the disaggregation even further. In examining the possibility of standardizing one product's packaging, for example, she found there were local issues about the type and color of the cap; the material used for the bottle; the size, shape, and color of the bottle; and the size of the label. Each item required a separate evaluation of costs and bene-

---

Disaggregating a Synergy Program

All too often, executives set overly broad goals for their synergy programs—goals that make good slogans but provide little guidance to managers in the field. By disaggregating a broad goal into more precisely defined objectives, managers will be better able to evaluate cost and benefits and, when appropriate, create concrete implementation plans. Here we see how one broad and ill-defined goal—"leveraging international brands"—was systematically broken down into meaningful components that could be addressed individually.

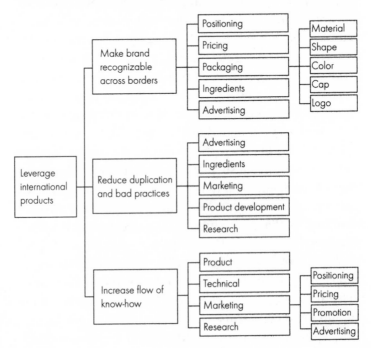

fits. The type of cap, for example, had a big impact on manufacturing costs—and thus was an attractive candidate for standardization—but some local managers argued that changes in cap design could hinder their marketing efforts. Customers in different countries preferred different cap mechanisms. By carefully balancing the cost savings from economies of scale in manufacturing against the possible loss of sales, the category manager and the local managers were able to reach a consensus on how much to reduce cap variety.

By disaggregating the objectives, the category manager was also able to gain a better understanding of how each effort should be implemented. Standardizing bottle shapes across countries, for example, would require a corporate policy. Otherwise, many of the local managers would go their own way, and economies of scale would be lost. Increasing the flow of technical know-how, by contrast, would be best achieved simply by creating better lines of communication among the technicians in each country. More heavy-handed, top-down initiatives would risk making technical managers resentful and could end up dampening rather than promoting efforts to share expertise.

Once the overall synergy goal has been broken down into its main components, the next step should be to estimate the size of the net benefit in each area. Uncertainties about both the costs and the benefits, however, often lead executives to avoid this obvious task. But without some concrete sense of the payoff, the decision maker will be forced to act on instinct rather than reason. That does not mean that an exhaustive financial analysis has to be performed before anything gets done. In most cases, order-of-magnitude estimates will do. Is the program likely to deliver $1 million, $10 million, or

$100 million in added profits? Is the impact on return on sales likely to be half a percentage point, or one percentage point, or five? This is back-of-the-envelope stuff, but we have found that even such rough estimates promote the kind of objective thinking that counters the biases.

The estimated financial benefits don't always tell the whole story, though. They rarely take into full account the opportunity costs of a synergy program, particularly the costs that result from not focusing management's time and effort elsewhere. The difficulty lies in knowing when the opportunity costs are likely to be greater than the benefits. At one consumer-products company, for example, the corporate center was spearheading an initiative to take a product that had been successful in one country and roll it out in a number of other countries. The local managers resisted the idea. They argued that the program would incur considerable opportunity costs, forcing them to divert marketing funds and management time from other local brands. The key to resolving the dispute lay in determining the strategic importance of the planned rollout.

If the rollout was strategically important, either to the units involved or to the overall corporation, then the benefits would likely outweigh the opportunity costs. But if some other more strategically important initiative was likely to be delayed in order to implement the rollout, then the opportunity costs would be greater. After some soul-searching by the units and by corporate marketing, it was agreed that the rollout had low strategic importance, except in three units. Headquarters scaled back the initiative. It would give advice and support to those units that wanted to go ahead with the product launch, but it would not impose a rollout on the other units.

Sizing the prize provides a counterweight to the synergy bias, forcing corporate managers to substantiate their assumptions that the synergy initiatives they propose will create big net benefits. It also helps counter the parenting bias, as the careful analysis of opportunity costs can help corporate managers better understand the source of any unit manager's resistance. And, by leading to the disaggregation of broad initiatives into discrete, well-defined programs, sizing the prize can set the stage for a focused, successful implementation.

Pinpointing the Parenting Opportunity

Even when a synergy prize is found to be sizable, corporate executives should not necessarily rush in. We would in general urge a cautious approach unless the need for corporate intervention is clear and compelling. Corporate executives should start with the assumption that when it makes good commercial sense, the business-unit managers will usually cooperate without the need for corporate involvement.

When is intervention by the corporate parent justified? Only when corporate executives can, first, point to a specific problem that is preventing the unit managers from working together; second, show why their involvement would solve the problem; and third, confirm that they have the skills required to get the job done. In those circumstances, there is what we call a *parenting opportunity*. We have found that genuine parenting opportunities tend to take four forms:

Even when a synergy prize is found to be sizable, corporate executives should not necessarily rush in.

Perception opportunities arise when businesses are unaware of the potential benefits of synergy. The oversight may be caused by a lack of interest, a lack of information, or a lack of personal contacts. The parent can help fill the perception gap by, for example, disseminating important information or by introducing aggressive performance targets that encourage units to look to other units for better ways to operate.

In general, the greater the number of business units in a company, the more likely it is that perception opportunities will arise. ABB, for example, has 5,000 profit centers organized into a number of business areas. In its power transformer area alone, there are more than 30 units. It is clearly impractical for every unit head to know what is going on in each of the other 29 units. The cost of scanning is too high. The area head, therefore, plays an important role in facilitating the information flow, passing on best-practice ideas and introducing managers to one another. In addition, the area head regularly publishes financial and operating information about each business, enabling cross-unit comparisons and helping each business identify units from which it can learn useful lessons.

Evaluation opportunities arise when the businesses fail to assess correctly the costs and benefits of a potential synergy. The businesses' judgments may be biased by previous experiences with similar initiatives, distorted by shortcomings in the processes or methods they use to assess cost-benefit trade-offs, or skewed by their own strategic priorities. In such cases, the parent should play a role in correcting the units' thinking.

The German subsidiary of one multinational company, for example, was fiercely protective of a new product it had developed. It was not only reluctant to help other units develop similar products, it even refused visits from unit and corporate-center technicians. The reason? The German managers did not trust their French and Italian colleagues to price the new product appropriately. They feared those units would not position it as a premium product and, as a result, would undermine price levels throughout Europe, reducing the exceptional profits being generated in the German market. The Germans' fear of the possible downsides clouded their view of the very real upsides. The standoff was resolved only when corporate executives walked the German managers through the cost-benefit calculations step by step and guaranteed that prices would be kept above a certain minimum in all countries.

Motivation opportunities, which derive from a simple lack of enthusiasm by one or more units, can stop collaboration dead in its tracks. Disincentives come in a number of forms. Unit managers may, for example, believe that the personal costs of cooperating are too high—that their personal empires or bonuses may be put at risk. Or transfer-pricing mechanisms may, in effect, penalize one unit for cooperating with another. Or two unit managers may simply dislike each other, preventing them from working together constructively. Identifying and removing motivational roadblocks, whether they reside in measurement and reward systems or in interpersonal relations, can be one of the toughest, but most valuable, roles for the corporate executive.

Any decision for parental intervention should also take account of the skills of the managers involved.

In one company, the CEO tried for five years to get the managers responsible for North American and European operations to cooperate. The North American business was run by a headstrong young woman with a strong belief in an open management style. Europe was run by a reserved, traditional Englishman who preferred to operate through formal, hierarchical structures. Both managers privately aspired to run the entire global business, but publicly they argued that there were few overlaps between their businesses that would merit collaboration. After a series of failed attempts to get the businesses to work together, each of which ended in bitter rows and recriminations, the CEO finally lost patience and fired both managers. In their places, he appointed more compatible managers who were able to work together with a great deal of success.

Implementation opportunities open up when unit managers understand and commit to a synergy program but, through a lack of skills, people, or other resources, can't make it happen. The business heads of a European chemical company, for example, agreed that it would be valuable to pool their resources when setting up an Asia-Pacific office in Singapore. Their aim was to improve the effectiveness of their sales efforts in markets that were unfamiliar to all of them. The initiative failed because none of the businesses had a suitable candidate to head the office; the individual appointed was not well connected in the region and lacked the skills needed to open new accounts. If the parent had intervened, by providing a suitable manager from its central staff or training and by coaching the man appointed, the chances of success would have increased greatly.

Thinking through the nature of the parenting opportunity, and hence the role that the parent needs to play, helps corporate executives pinpoint which type of intervention, if any, makes sense. But any decision to intervene should also take account of the skills of the managers involved. Appointing a purchasing specialist to advise the businesses on gaining leverage by pooling their purchases may be an excellent idea, but if the parent does not have the right person to do the job, the new appointment will end up irritating and alienating the businesses. A lack of the right skills can thwart even the best of intentions.

The discipline of pinpointing the parenting opportunity is probably the most valuable contribution that we have to offer to corporate executives in search of synergy. Thinking clearly about why parental intervention is needed can help managers avoid mirages and select suitable interventions. Unless a parenting opportunity can be pinpointed, our advice is not to intervene at all.

Bringing Downsides to Light

The synergy is attractive; the parenting opportunity is clear; the skills are in place. Is it time to act? Not necessarily. A final discipline is in order: looking carefully for any collateral damage that may occur from the synergy program. Because the pursuit of synergy affects the relationship among business units and the relationship between the units and the corporate center—two of the most sensitive relationships in any big company—it can have far-reaching consequences for a company's organization and strategy. If corporate executives overlook the negative knock-on effects, they risk great harm.

Some synergy efforts send the wrong signals to line managers and employees, clouding their understanding of corporate priorities and damaging the credibility of headquarters. When one company set up a coordination committee to seek marketing synergies among its businesses, the unit managers thought the CEO was abandoning his much-communicated goal of promoting stronger accountability at the individual unit level. They saw the corporate committee as a sign of a return to more centralized control. In fact, the shift of accountability to the units remained a core strategic thrust—the synergy initiative was simply a tactical effort intended to save money. In another company, an initiative to coordinate back-office functions distracted employees from the corporation's fundamental strategic goal of becoming more focused on the customer. They began looking inward rather than outward.

Top-down synergy efforts can also undermine employee motivation and innovation. One consumer-goods company, for example, launched an effort to coordinate research and development across its European units. Although the effort appeared to be highly attractive, offering substantial productivity gains, it backfired. A key source of innovation in the company had been the internal competition between the U.K. and the Continental businesses. By establishing a combined research unit, headquarters ended the competition—and the creativity. The effort succeeded in eliminating duplicated effort and achieving economies of scale, but these gains were overshadowed by the unanticipated downsides.

In other cases, cooperation can distort the way unit managers think about their business, leading to wrong-headed decisions. Consider the experience of a diversified retailing company that tried to encourage greater cooperation between its two appliance-retailing businesses. One of the businesses, which focused on selling top-quality appliances at premium prices, was highly profitable. The other, which pursued a pile-it-high, sell-it-cheap strategy, was barely breaking even. The group CEO recognized the differences between the businesses, but he felt certain that synergy could be achieved, particularly in purchasing. To encourage greater cooperation, he put the head of the profitable business in charge of both operations.

The new leader of the two business units initially looked for areas where purchases could be pooled to gain greater leverage over suppliers. But although some small cost reductions were quickly realized, the program soon ran into difficulty: the two businesses were buying different kinds of products, with different price points and different proportions of store-branded items. It was clear that big savings could only be achieved if the two businesses bought identical products. The managers of the struggling unit initially resisted this course, but as they learned more about the product and pricing strategies of their more successful partner, their thinking began to change. Entranced by the wide margins available from selling premium goods, they began shifting their strategy. They bought better-quality products, boosted service levels, and raised prices.

The result was calamitous. The unit's traditional, price-conscious customers went elsewhere for their bargains, while upmarket purchasers stuck with their traditional suppliers. In emulating its sister company, the unit had undermined its business. It had tried to take its product mix upscale without taking account of its competitive positioning. The new strategy was soon reversed, but it took more than a year to remove the inappropriate products from the supply chain. The unit suffered big losses and major write-offs.

It is never possible to predict all the unintended consequences that can flow from a synergy initiative (or, for that matter, from any management action). But by simply being aware that business-unit collaboration can have big downsides, managers will be able to take a more objective, rigorous view of potential synergy efforts. In some cases, they will be able to structure the effort to avoid many of the potential downsides. In other cases, they will be able to kill proposals that would have created more problems than they solved.

First, Do No Harm

Managers have sometimes accused us of being too skeptical about synergy. They argue that the disciplined approach we recommend—clarifying the real benefits to be gained, examining the potential for parental involvement, taking into account the possible downsides—will mean that fewer initiatives will be launched. And they are right. We believe that corporate managers should be more selective in their synergy interventions. In all too many companies, synergy programs are considered nobrainers. Cooperation and sharing are viewed as ideals that are beyond debate. As we've seen, such assumptions often lead to failed initiatives that waste time and money and, sometimes, severely damage businesses. Real synergy opportunities exist in most large companies, but they are rarely as plentiful as executives assume. The challenge is to distinguish the valid opportunities from the mirages. (See the exhibit "A Disciplined Approach to Synergy.")

In some cases, the analysis of synergy opportunities will raise questions that will be hard to answer. The size of the prize may be uncertain: Will a joint Internet marketing group help or hinder our businesses as they move into electronic commerce? The parenting opportunity may be unclear: Is the German product manager resisting the corporate marketing campaign out of chauvinistic stubbornness, or is the German market really different? The needed skills may be unproven: Will our

A Disciplined Approach to Synergy

By taking a more disciplined approach to achieving synergy, an executive can gain its rewards while avoiding its frustrations. The first step is to evaluate the costs and benefits—to "size the prize." If the net benefit is unclear, more exploration is needed. If it appears to be small, the executive should not pursue the synergy unless the risks of corporate intervention are low. If it seems large, the executive should determine whether an intervention by the corporate parent makes sense. If the parenting opportunity is unclear, the intervention should be restricted to facilitating further exploration. If no parenting opportunity exists, the executive should resist any urge to intervene. If a clear parenting opportunity exists, the executive should tailor the intervention to fit the opportunity while minimizing any downside risks.

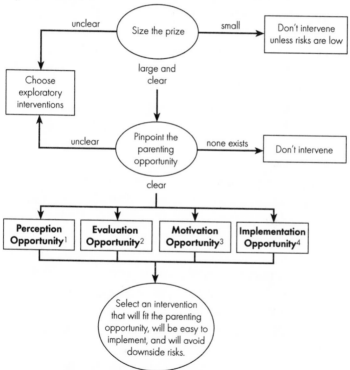

Notes: 1. Units are unable to perceive the synergy or its benefits.
      2. Units do not accurately evaluate the benefit.
      3. Disincentives are preventing the units from pursuing the synergy.
      4. Units lack skills, resources, or processes to achieve the synergy.

technical manager be able to lead a coordination committee on production planning? The risks may be hard to pin down: Will a cross-Asian product-development group undermine innovation?

When uncertainty is high, we recommend that corporate executives proceed cautiously. Rather than intervene decisively, they should encourage further exploration. The mechanisms for exploration may be similar to those for implementation—pilot projects, fact-finding visits, temporary assignments and task forces, forums for sharing ideas—but they are very different in intent. An exploratory mechanism is designed simply to collect facts. The end result is a better-informed decision maker. In implementation mode, by contrast, the intention is to change the way managers are working or thinking.

Sometimes, the best course will be to do nothing. The opportunity may be too small to justify the expenditure of management time, there may be no clear reason for the parent to intervene, or the risks may be too high. The thought of doing nothing will, of course, make many executives distinctly uncomfortable. After all, it goes against the grain of the most basic managerial instincts: to take action, to get things done, to create a whole greater than the sum of the parts. Yet executives who are not prepared to countenance a do-nothing outcome should ask themselves whether they are in the throes of biased thinking.

When executives manage synergy well, it can be a boon, creating additional value with existing resources.

If convinced that the benefit is sizable and the parenting opportunity real, executives can then search for the best kind of corporate intervention. There are usually several possible choices, all with different advantages and drawbacks. Synergies from combined purchasing power, for example, might be achieved by centralizing purchasing, by setting up a purchasing coordination committee, by establishing a corporate advisory center, by creating a cross-unit database on purchases, or by setting corporate standards for terms and conditions. The decision on how to intervene should depend on the nature of the benefit and the parenting opportunity. But it should also take into account the available skills in the organization and the ease with which implementation is likely to take place. And it should seek to minimize the downside risks. Carefully selected interventions are the best way to release truly valuable synergy.

When synergy is well managed, it can be a boon, creating additional value with existing resources. But when it's poorly managed, it can undermine an organization's confidence and erode the trust among business units as well as between the units and the corporate center. Synergy's upsides are real, but so are its downsides. And the only way for managers to avoid the downsides is to rid themselves of the biases that cloud their thinking. When it comes to synergy, executives would be wise to heed the physicians' creed: First, do no harm.

What Is Synergy?

THE WORD SYNERGY is derived from the Greek word *synergos,* which means "working together." In business usage, synergy refers to the ability of two or more units or companies to generate greater value working together than they could working apart. We've found that most business synergies take one of six forms:

Shared Know-How

Units often benefit from sharing knowledge or skills. They may, for example, improve their results by pooling their insights into a particular process, function, or geographic area. The know-how they share may be written in manuals or in policy-and-procedure statements, but very often it exists tacitly, without formal documentation. Value can be created simply by exposing one set of people to another who have a different way of getting things done. The emphasis that many companies place on leveraging core competencies and sharing best practices reflects the importance attributed to shared know-how.

Coordinated Strategies

It sometimes works to a company's advantage to align the strategies of two or more of its businesses. Divvying up markets among units may, for instance, reduce interunit competition. And coordinating responses to shared competitors may be a powerful and effective way to counter competitive threats. Although coordinated strategies can in principle be an important source of synergy, they're tough to achieve. Striking the right balance between corporate intervention and business-unit autonomy is not easy.

Shared Tangible Resources

Units can sometimes save a lot of money by sharing physical assets or resources. By using a common manufacturing facility or research laboratory, for example, they may gain econo-mies of scale and avoid duplicated effort. Companies often justify acquisitions of related businesses by pointing to the synergies to be gained from sharing resources.

Vertical Integration

Coordinating the flow of products or services from one unit to another can reduce inventory costs, speed product development, increase capacity utilization, and improve market access. In process industries such as petrochemicals and forest products, well-managed vertical integration can yield particularly large benefits.

Pooled Negotiating Power

By combining their purchases, different units can gain greater leverage over suppliers, reducing the cost or even improving the quality of the goods they buy. Companies can also gain similar benefits by negotiating jointly with other stakeholders, such as customers, governments, or universities. The gains from pooled negotiating power can be dramatic.

Combined Business Creation

The creation of new businesses can be facilitated by combining know-how from different units, by extracting discrete activities from various units and combining them in a new unit, or by establishing internal joint ventures or alliances. As a result of the business world's increased concern for corporate regeneration and growth, several companies have placed added emphasis on this type of synergy.

Originally published in September–October 1998
Reprint 98504

The End of
Corporate Imperialism

C.K. PRAHALAD AND

KENNETH LIEBERTHAL

Executive Summary

AS THEY SEARCH FOR GROWTH, multinational corporations will have no choice but to compete in the big emerging markets of China, India, Indonesia, and Brazil. But while it is still common to question how corporations will change life in those markets, Western executives would be smart to turn the question around. The authors assert that the multinationals themselves will be transformed by their experience. In fact, they say, MNCs will have to rethink every element of their business models in order to be successful.

During the first wave of market entry in the 1980s, MNCs operated with what might be termed an imperialist mind-set. They assumed, for example, that the big emerging markets would be new markets for their old products. As a result of this mind-set, multinationals have achieved only limited success in these markets.

The authors guide readers through five questions that companies must answer to compete effectively. First and foremost, MNCs must define the emerging middle-class markets—which are significantly different from those in the West—and determine a business model that will serve their needs.

The transformation that multinationals must undergo is not cosmetic—simply developing greater cultural sensitivity will not do the trick. In order to compete in the big emerging markets, multinationals must reconfigure their resource base, rethink their cost structure, redesign their product development process, and challenge their assumptions about the cultural mix of their top-level managers. MNCs that recognize the need for such changes will likely reap the rewards of the postimperialist age.

As they search for growth, multinational corporations will have to compete in the big emerging markets of China, India, Indonesia, and Brazil. The operative word is *emerging*. A vast consumer base of hundreds of millions of people is developing rapidly. Despite the uncertainty and the difficulty of doing business in markets that remain opaque to outsiders, Western MNCs will have no choice but to enter them. (See the table "Market Size: Emerging Markets versus the United States.")

During the first wave of market entry in the 1980s, MNCs operated with what might be termed an imperialist mind-set. They assumed that the big emerging markets were new markets for their old products. They foresaw a bonanza in incremental sales for their existing products or the chance to squeeze profits out of their sunset technologies. Further, the corporate center was seen as the sole locus of product and process innovation.

A focus on incremental volume misses the real opportunity in emerging markets.

Many multinationals did not consciously look at emerging markets as sources of technical and managerial talent for their global operations. As a result of this imperialist mind-set, multinationals have achieved only limited success in those markets.

Many corporations, however, are beginning to see that the opportunity that big emerging markets represent will demand a new way of thinking. Success will require more than simply developing greater cultural sensitivity. The more we understand the nature of these markets, the more we believe that multinationals will have to rethink and reconfigure every element of their business models.

So while it is still common today to question how corporations like General Motors and McDonald's will change life in the big emerging markets, Western executives would be smart to turn the question around. Suc-

---

Market Size: Emerging Markets versus the United States

Product	China	India	Brazil	United States
Television (million units)	13.6	5.2	7.8	23.0
Detergent (kilograms per person)	2.5	2.7	7.3	14.4
(million tons)	3.5	2.3	1.1	3.9
Shampoo (in billions of dollars)	1.0	0.8	1.0	1.5
Pharmaceuticals (in billions of dollars)	5.0	2.8	8.0	60.6
Automotive (million units)	1.6	0.7	2.1	15.5
Power (megawatt capacity)	236,542	81,736	59,950	810,964

cess in the emerging markets will require innovation and resource shifts on such a scale that life within the multinationals themselves will inevitably be transformed. In short, as MNCs achieve success in those markets, they will also bring corporate imperialism to an end.

We would not like to give the impression that we think markets such as China, India, Brazil, and Indonesia will enjoy clear sailing. As Indonesia is showing, these markets face major obstacles to continued high growth; political disruptions, for example, can slow down and even reverse trends toward more open markets. But given the long-term growth prospects, MNCs will have to compete in those markets. Having studied in-depth the evolution of India and China over the past 20 years, and having worked extensively with MNCs competing in these and other countries, we believe that there are five basic questions that MNCs must answer to compete in the big emerging markets:

- Who is the emerging middle-class market in these countries, and what kind of business model will effectively serve their needs?

- What are the key characteristics of the distribution networks in these markets, and how are the networks evolving?

- What mix of local and global leadership is required to foster business opportunities?

- Should the MNC adopt a consistent strategy for all its business units within one country?

- Will local partners accelerate the multinational's ability to learn about the market?

What Is the Business Model for the Emerging Middle Class?

What is big and emerging in countries like China and India is a new consumer base consisting of hundreds of millions of people. Starved of choice for over 40 years, the rising middle class is hungry for consumer goods and a better quality of life and is ready to spend. The emerging markets have entered a new era of product availability and choice. In India alone, there are 50 brands of toothpaste available today and more than 250 brands of shoes.

Consumers are experimenting and changing their choice of products rapidly. Indians, for example, will buy any product once, but brand switching is common. One survey found that Indian consumers tried on average 6.2 brands of the same packaged-goods product in one year, compared with 2.0 for American consumers. But does this growth of consumer demand add up to a wealth of opportunity for the MNCs?

The answer is yes . . . but. Consider the constitution of the middle class itself. When managers in the West hear about the emerging middle class of India or China, they tend to think in terms of the middle class in Europe or the United States. This is one sign of an imperialist mind-set—the assumption that everyone must be just like "us." True, consumers in the emerging markets today are much more affluent than they were before their countries liberalized trade, but they are not affluent by Western standards. This is usually the first big miscalculation that MNCs make.

When these markets are analyzed, moreover, they turn out to have a structure very unlike that of the West. Income levels that characterize the Western middle class would represent a tiny upper class of consumers in any of the emerging markets. Today the active consumer market in the big emerging markets has a three-tiered pyramid structure. (See the exhibit "The Market Pyramid in China, India, and Brazil.")

Consider India. At the top of the pyramid, in tier one, is a relatively small number of consumers who are responsive to international brands and have the income to afford them. Next comes tier two, a much larger group of people who are less attracted to international brands. Finally, at the bottom of the pyramid of consumers is tier three—a massive group that is loyal to local customs, habits, and often to local brands. Below that is another huge group made up of people who are unlikely to become active consumers anytime soon.

MNCs have tended to bring their existing products and marketing strategies to the emerging markets without properly accounting for these market pyramids.

The Market Pyramid in China, India, and Brazil

	Purchasing power parity in U.S. dollars	China	India	Brazil
tier 1	greater than $20,000	2	7	9
tier 2	$10,000 to $20,000	60	63	15
tier 3	$5,000 to $10,000	330	125	27
	less than $5,000	800	700	105

Population in millions

They end up, therefore, becoming high-end niche players. That's what happened to Revlon, for example, when it introduced its Western beauty products to China in 1976 and to India in 1994. Only the top tier valued and could afford the cachet of Revlon's brand. And consider Ford's recent foray into India with its Escort, which Ford priced at more than $21,000. In India, anything over $20,000 falls into the luxury segment. The most popular car, the Maruti-Suzuki, sells for $10,000 or less. Fiat learned to serve that tier of the market in Brazil, designing a new model called the Palio specifically for Brazilians. Fiat is now poised to transfer that success from Brazil to India.

While it is seductive for companies like Ford to think of big emerging markets as new outlets for old products, a mind-set focused on incremental volume misses the real opportunity. To date, MNCs like Ford and Revlon have either ignored tier two of the pyramid or conceded it to local competitors. But if Ford wants to be more than a small, high-end player, it will have to design a robust and roomy $9,000 car to compete with Fiat's Palio or with a locally produced car.

Tailoring products to the big emerging markets is not a trivial task. Minor cultural adaptations or marginal cost reductions will not do the job. Instead, to overcome an implicit imperialism, companies must undergo a fundamental rethinking of every element of their business model.

RETHINKING THE PRICE-PERFORMANCE EQUATION

Consumers in big emerging markets are getting a fast education in global standards, but they often are unwilling to pay global prices. In India, an executive in a multinational food-processing company told us the story of a man in Delhi who went to McDonald's for a hamburger. He didn't like the food or the prices, but he liked the ambience. Then he went to Nirula's, a successful Delhi food chain. He liked the food and the prices there, but he complained to the manager because Nirula's did not have the same pleasant atmosphere as McDonald's. The moral of the story? Price-performance expectations are changing, often to the consternation of both the multinationals and the locals. McDonald's has been forced to adapt its menu to local tastes by adding vegetable burgers. Local chains like Nirula's have been pushed to meet global standards for cleanliness and ambience.

Consumers in the big emerging markets are far more focused than their Western counterparts on the price-performance equation. That focus tends to give low-cost local competitors the edge in hotly contested markets. MNCs can, however, learn to turn this price sensitivity to their advantage.

Philips Electronics, for example, introduced a combination video-CD player in China in 1994. Although there is virtually no market for this product in Europe or the United States, the Chinese quickly embraced it as a great two-for-one bargain. More than 15 million units have been sold in China, and the product seems likely to catch on in Indonesia and India. Consumers in those countries see the player as good value for the money.

RETHINKING BRAND MANAGEMENT

Armed with powerful, established brands, multinationals are likely to overestimate the extent of Westernization in the emerging markets and the value of using a consistent approach to brand management around the world.

In India, Coca-Cola overvalued the pull of its brand among the tier-two consumers. Coke based its advertising strategy on its worldwide image and then watched the advantage slip to Pepsi, which had adopted a campaign that was oriented toward the Indian market. As one of Coke's senior executives recently put it in the *Wall Street Journal*, "We're so successful in international business that we applied a tried and true formula . . . and it was the wrong formula to apply in India."

It took Coke more than two years to get the message, but it is now repositioning itself by using local heroes, such as popular cricket players, in its advertising. Perhaps more important, it is heavily promoting a popular Indian brand of cola—Thums Up—which Coke bought from a local bottler in 1993, only to scorn it for several years as a poor substitute for the Real Thing.

RETHINKING THE COSTS OF MARKET BUILDING

For many MNCs, entering an emerging market means introducing a new product or service category. But Kellogg, for example, found that introducing breakfast cereals to India was a slow process because it meant creating new eating habits. Once the company had persuaded Indians to eat cereal, at great expense, local competitors were able to ride on Kellogg's coattails by introducing breakfast cereals with local flavors. As a result, Kellogg may discover in the long run that they paid too high a price for too small a market. Sampling, celebrity

endorsements, and other forms of consumer education
are expensive: regional tastes vary and language barriers
can create difficulties. India, for example, has 13 major
languages and pronounced cultural differences across
regions.

Multinationals would do well to rethink the costs of
building markets. Changing developed habits is difficult
and expensive. Providing consumers with a new product
that requires no reeducation can be much easier. For
example, consider the rapid adoption of pagers in China.
Because telephones are not widely available there,
pagers have helped fill the void as a means of one-way
communication.

RETHINKING PRODUCT DESIGN

Even when consumers in emerging markets appear to
want the same products as are sold elsewhere, some
redesign is often necessary to reflect differences in use,
distribution, or selling. Because the Chinese use pagers
to send entire messages—which is not how they were
intended to be used—Motorola developed pagers capable of displaying more lines of information. The result:
Motorola encountered the enviable problem of having to
scramble to keep up with exploding demand for its
product.

In the mid-1980s, a leading MNC in telecommunications began exporting its electronic switching systems to
China for use in the phone system. The switching systems had been designed for the company's home market, where there were many customers but substantial
periods when the phones were not in use. In China, on
the other hand, there were very few phones, but they

were in almost constant use. The switching system, which worked flawlessly in the West, simply couldn't handle the load in China. Ultimately, the company had to redesign its software.

Distribution can also have a huge impact on product design. A Western maker of frozen desserts, for example, had to reformulate one of its products not because of differences in consumers' tastes, but because the refrigerators in most retail outlets in India weren't cold enough to store the product properly. The product had been designed for storage at minus 15 degrees centigrade, but the typical retailer's refrigerator operates at minus 4 degrees. Moreover, power interruptions frequently shut down the refrigerators.

RETHINKING PACKAGING

Whether the problem is dust, heat, or bumpy roads, the distribution infrastructure in emerging markets places special strains on packaging. One glass manufacturer, for example, was stunned at the breakage it sustained as a result of poor roads and trucks in India.

And consumers in tiers two and three are likely to have packaging preferences that are different from consumers in the West. Single-serve packets, or sachets, are enormously popular in India. They allow consumers to buy only what they need, experiment with new products, and conserve cash at the same time. Products as varied as detergents, shampoos, pickles, cough syrup, and oil are sold in sachets in India, and it is estimated that they make up 20% to 30% of the total sold in their categories. Sachets are spreading as a marketing device for such items as shampoos in China as well.

RETHINKING CAPITAL EFFICIENCY

The common wisdom is that the infrastructure problems in emerging markets—inefficient distribution systems, poor banking facilities, and inadequate logistics—will require companies to use more capital than in Western markets, not less. But that is the wrong mindset. Hindustan Lever, a subsidiary of Unilever in India, saw a low-cost Indian detergent maker, Nirma, become the largest branded detergent maker in the world over a seven-year period by courting the tier-two and tier-three markets. Realizing that it could not compete by making marginal changes, Hindustan Lever rethought every aspect of its business, including production, distribution, marketing, and capital efficiency.

Today Hindustan Lever operates a $2 billion business with effectively zero working capital. Consider just one of the practices that makes this possible. The company keeps a supply of signed checks from its dealers. When it ships an order, it simply writes in the correct amount for the order. This practice is not uncommon in India. The Indian agribusiness company, Rallis, uses it with its 20,000 dealers in rural India. But this way of doing things is unheard of in Unilever's home countries, the United Kingdom and the Netherlands.

Hindustan Lever also manages to operate with minimal fixed capital. It does so in part through an active program of supplier management; the company works with local entrepreneurs who own and manage plants whose capacity is dedicated to Hindustan Lever's products. Other MNCs will find that there is less need for vertical integration in emerging markets than they might think. Quality suppliers can be located and developed.

Their lower overhead structure can help the MNCs gain a competitive cost position. Supply chain management is an important tool for changing the capital efficiency of a multinational's operations.

Rather than concede the market, Hindustan Lever radically changed itself and is today successfully competing against Nirma with a low-cost detergent called Wheel. The lesson learned in India has not been lost on Unilever. It is unlikely to concede tier-two and tier-three markets in China, Indonesia, or Brazil without a fight.

How Does the Distribution System Work?

One of the greatest regrets of multinational executives, especially those we spoke with in China, was that they had not invested more in distribution before launching their products. Access to distribution is often critical to success in emerging markets, and it cannot be taken for granted. There is no

In India, entrepreneurs have put together a national distribution system in many businesses.

substitute for a detailed understanding of the unique characteristics of a market's distribution system and how that system is likely to evolve.

Consider the differences between China and India. Distribution in China is primarily local and provincial. Under the former planned economy, most distribution networks were confined to political units, such as counties, cities, or provinces. Even at present, there is no real national distribution network for most products. Many MNCs have gained access to provincial networks by creating joint ventures. But these JVs are now impediments to the creation of the badly needed national network. Chinese JV partners protect their turf. This gap between the MNCs' need for a national, cost-effective distribution system and the more locally oriented goals of their partners is creating serious tensions. We expect that many JVs formed originally to allow multinationals market and distribution access will be restructured because of this very issue during the next five to seven years.

In India, on the other hand, individual entrepreneurs have already put together a national distribution system in a wide variety of businesses. Established companies such as Colgate-Palmolive and Godrej in personal care, Hindustan Lever in packaged goods, Tatas in trucks, Bajaj in scooters—the list is long—control their own distribution systems. Those systems take the form of long-standing arrangements with networks of small-scale distributors throughout the country, and the banking network is part of those relationships. Many of the established packaged-goods companies reach more than 3 million retail outlets—using trains, trucks, bullock-drawn carts, camels, and bicycles. And many companies claim to service each one of those outlets once a week.

Any MNC that wants to establish its own distribution system in India inevitably runs up against significant obstacles and costs. Ford, for example, is trying to establish a new, high-quality dealer network to sell cars in India. To obtain a dealership, each prospective dealer is expected to invest a large amount of his own money and must undergo special training. In the long haul, Ford's approach may prove to be a major source of advantage to the company, but the cost in cash and managerial attention of building the dealers' network will be substantial.

Ironically, the lack of a national distribution system in China may be an advantage. MNCs with patience and ingenuity can more easily build distribution systems to suit their needs, and doing so might confer competitive advantages. As one manager we talked to put it, "The trick to sustained, long-term profitability in China lies not in technology or in savvy advertising or even in low pricing, but rather in building a modern distribution system." Conceivably, China may see consolidation of the retail market earlier than India.

The Chinese and Indian cases signal the need for MNCs to develop a market-specific distribution strategy. In India, MNCs will have to determine who controls national distribution in order to distinguish likely partners from probable competitors. In China, multinationals seeking national distribution of their products must consider the motivations of potential partners before entering relationships that may frustrate their intentions.

Will Local or Expatriate Leadership Be More Effective?

Leadership of a multinational's venture in an emerging market requires a complex blend of local sensitivity and global knowledge. Getting the balance right is critical but never easy. MNCs frequently lack the cultural understanding to get the mix of expatriate and local leaders right.

Expatriates from the MNCs' host country play multiple roles. They transfer technology and management practices. They ensure that local employees understand and practice the corporate culture. In the early stages of market development, expatriates are the conduits for information flow between the multinational's corporate office and the local operation. But while headquarters staff usually recognizes the importance of sending information to the local operation, they tend to be less aware that information must also be received from the other direction. Expatriates provide credibility at headquarters when they convey information, especially information concerning the adaptations the corporation must make in order to be successful in the emerging market. Given these important roles, the large number of expatriates in China—170,000 by one count—is understandable.

Every multinational operation we observed in China had several expatriates in management positions. In India, by contrast, we rarely saw expatriate managers, and the few that we did see were usually of Indian origin. That's because among the big emerging markets, India is unique in that it has developed, over time, a cadre of engineers and managers.

MNCs frequently lack the cultural understanding to get the mix of expatriate and local leaders right.

The Indian institutes of technology and institutes of management turn out graduates with a high degree of technical competence.

Perhaps more important from the perspective of a multinational, Indian managers speak English fluently and seem adept at learning a new corporate culture. At the same time, they have a much better appreciation of local nuances and a deeper commitment to the Indian market than any expatriate could have.

Those seeming advantages may be offset, however, by two disadvantages. First, a management team of native-born managers may not have the same "share of voice" at corporate headquarters that expatriate managers have. Yet maintaining a strong voice is essential, given the difficulty most managers at corporate headquarters have in understanding the dynamics and peculiar requirements of operating in emerging markets. Second, the "soft technology" that is central to Western competitive advantage—the bundle of elements that creates a dynamic, cost-effective, market-sensitive organization—is hard to develop when the management team consists of people who have worked only briefly, if at all, in such an organization.

Several multinationals have sent expatriates of Chinese or Indian origin from their U.S. or European base back to their Chinese or Indian operations in order to convey the company's soft technology in a culturally sensitive way. But that strategy has not, in general, been successful. As one manager we spoke to noted, "Indians from the United States who are sent back as expatriates are frozen in time. They remember the India they left 20 years ago. They are totally out of sync. But they do not have the humility to accept that they have to learn." We heard the same sentiment echoed in China, both for Chinese-Americans and, less frequently, for Chinese who had obtained a higher education in the United States and then returned as a part of a multinational management team.

Using American or West European expatriates during the early years of market entry can make sense, but this approach has its own set of problems. Cultural and language difficulties in countries like China and India typically limit expats' interaction with the locals as well as their effectiveness. In addition, the need to understand how to deal with the local political system, especially in China, makes long-term assignments desirable. It often takes an expatriate manager two years to get fully up to speed. From the company's perspective, it makes sense to keep that manager in place for another three years to take full advantage of what he or she has learned. But few Western expatriates are willing to stay in China that long; many feel that a long assignment keeps them out of the loop and may impose a high career cost. Multinationals, therefore, need to think about how to attract and retain high-quality expatriate talent, how to maintain expats' links to the parent company, and how to use and pass along expats' competencies once they move on to another post.

Is It Necessary to "Present One Face"?

Beyond the normal organizational questions that would exist wherever a company does business, there is a question of special importance in emerging markets: Do local political considerations require the multinational to adopt a uniform strategy for each of its business units operating in the country, or can it permit each unit to act on its own?

As with the issue of distribution, the contrasts between China and India make clear why there is no one right answer to this question. In China, massive governmental interference in the economy makes a uniform country strategy necessary. The

In China, government interference in the economy makes a uniform county strategy necessary.

Chinese government tends to view the activities of individual business units as part of a single company's effort, and therefore concessions made by any one unit—such as an agreement to achieve a certain level of local sourcing—may well become requirements for the others. An MNC in China must be able to articulate a set of principles that conforms to China's announced priorities, and it should coordinate the activities of its various business units so that they resonate with those priorities.

Given the way most multinationals operate, "presenting one face" to China is very difficult. Business units have their own P&L responsibilities and are reluctant to lose their autonomy. Reporting lines can become overly complex. Although we observed many organizational approaches, not a single MNC we looked at is completely satisfied with its approach to this difficult issue.

Is it any wonder? Consider the life of one MNC executive we visited in China. As the head of his company's China effort, he has to coordinate with the company's regional headquarters in Japan, report to international headquarters in Europe, and maintain close contact with corporate headquarters in North America. He also has to meet with members of the Chinese government, with the MNC's business-unit executives in China, and with the leaders of the business units' Chinese partners. Simply maintaining all of these contacts is extraordinarily taxing and time consuming.

There is somewhat less need to present one face to India. Since 1991, the Indian government has scaled back its efforts to shape what MNCs do in the country. Business units may therefore act more independently than would be appropriate in China. The strategy for India can be developed on a business-by-business basis. Nonetheless, the market is large and complex. National regulations are onerous, and state-level governments are still so different from one another that MNCs are well advised to develop knowledge that they can share with all their business units in India.

Do Partners Foster Valuable Learning?

In the first wave of market entry, multinationals used joint ventures extensively as a way not only to navigate through bureaucratic processes but also to learn about new markets. With few exceptions, however, JVs in emerging markets have been problematic. In some cases, executives of the multinationals mistakenly thought the JVs would do their strategic thinking for them. In most cases, tensions in JV relationships have diverted management attention away from learning about the market.

One consistent problem is that companies enter joint ventures with very different expectations. One Chinese manager described the situation in terms of an old saying: We are sleeping in the same bed, with different dreams. The local partner sees the MNC as a source of technology and investment, and the multinational sees the partner as a means to participate in the domestic market.

When they come to an emerging market, multinationals usually are still building their manufacturing and marketing infrastructures, and they don't expect immediate returns. Local partners, however, often want to see short-term profit. This disparity of aims leads to enormous strain in the relationship. The costs associated with expatriate managers also become a bone of contention. Who controls what can be yet another source of trouble—especially when the domestic partner has experience in the business. And when new investment is needed to grow the business, local partners often are unable to bring in the matching funds, yet they resent the dilution of their holding and the ensuing loss of control.

MNCs are finally learning that their local partners often do not have adequate market knowledge. The experience of most local partners predates the emergence of real consumer markets, and their business practices can be archaic. But as markets evolve toward greater transparency, as MNCs develop senior managers who understand how "the system" works, and as the availability of local talent increases, multinationals have less to gain by using intermediaries as a vehicle for learning.

The MNCs' need for local partners clearly is diminishing. In 1997, a consulting firm surveyed 67 companies invested in China and found that the percentage of their projects that became wholly foreign-owned enterprises grew steadily from 18% in 1992 to 37% in 1996. A *passive* partner that can provide a local face may still be important in some industries, but this is a very different matter from the JV.

Success Will Transform the Multinationals

As executives look for growth in the big emerging markets, they tend quite naturally to focus on the size of the opportunity and the challenges that lie ahead. Few, however, stop to think about how success will transform their companies. But consider the magnitude of the changes we have been describing and the sheer size of the markets in question. Success in the big emerging markets will surely change the shape of the modern multinational as we know it today.

For years, executives have assumed they could export their current business models around the globe. That assumption has to change. Citicorp, for example, aims to serve a billion banking customers by 2010. There is no way Citicorp, given its current cost structure, can profitably serve someone in Beijing or Delhi whose net wealth is less than $5,000. But if Citicorp creates a new business model—rethinking every element of its cost structure—it will be able to serve not only average Chinese people but also inner-city residents in New York. In short, companies must realize that the innovation required to serve the large tier-two and tier-three segments in emerging markets has the potential to make them more competitive in their traditional markets—and therefore in *all* markets.

Over time, the imperialist assumption that innovation comes from the center will gradually fade away and die. Increasingly, as multinationals develop products better adapted to the emerging markets, they are finding that those markets are becoming an important source of innovation. Telecommunications companies, for example, are discovering that people in markets with no old technology to "forget" may accept technological changes faster. MNCs such as Texas Instruments and Motorola are assigning responsibility for software-oriented business development to their Indian operations. China has become such a significant market for video-CD players that the Chinese are likely to be major players in introducing the next round of video-CD standards around the world.

The big emerging markets will also have a significant influence on the product development philosophy of the MNCs. One major multinational recognized to its surprise that the Chinese have found a way of producing high-quality detergents with equipment and processes that cost about one-fifth of what the MNC spends. Stories like that get repeated in a wide variety of businesses, including fine chemicals, cement, textile machinery, trucks, and television sets.

As product development becomes decentralized, collaboration between labs in Bangalore, London, and Dallas, for example, will gradually become the rule, not the exception. New-product introductions will have to take into consideration nontraditional centers of influence. Thus in the CD business at Philips, new-product introductions, which previously occurred almost exclusively in Europe, now also take place in Shanghai and California.

As corporate imperialism draws to a close, multinationals will increasingly look to emerging markets for talent. India is already recognized as a source of technical talent in engineering, sciences, and software, as well as in some aspects of management. All high-tech companies recruit in India not only for the Indian market but also for the global market. China, given its growth and its technical and managerial-training infrastructure, has not yet reached that stage, but it may well reach it in the not-too-distant future.

A major shift in geographical resources will take place within the next five years. Philips is already downsizing in Europe and reportedly employs more Chinese than Dutch workers. Over 40% of the market for Coke, Gillette, Lucent, Boeing, and GE power systems is in Asia.

How many multinationals are prepared to accommodate 30% to 40% of their top team coming from China, India, and Brazil?

And in the last two years, ABB has shrunk its European head count by more than 40,000 while adding 45,000 people in Asia.

In addition to these changes, an increasing percentage of the investment in plant and equipment and marketing will go to the emerging markets. As those markets grow to account for 30% to 40% of capital invested—and even a larger percentage of market share and profits—they will attract much more attention from top management.

The importance of these markets will inevitably be reflected in the ethnic and national origin of senior management. At present, with a few exceptions such as Citicorp and Unilever, senior management ranks are filled with nationals from the company's home country. By the year 2010, however, the top 200 managers from around the world for any multinational will have a much greater cultural and ethnic mix.

How many of today's multinationals are prepared to accommodate 30% to 40% of their top team of 200 coming from China, India, and Brazil? How will that cultural mix influence decision making, risk taking, and team building? Diversity will put an enormous burden on top-level managers to articulate clearly the values and behaviors expected of senior managers, and it will demand large investments in training and socialization. The need for a single company culture will also become more critical as people from different cultures begin to work together. Providing the right glue to hold companies together will be a big challenge.

That challenge will be intensified by an impending power shift within multinationals. The end of corporate imperialism suggests more than a new relationship between the developed and the emerging economies. It also suggests an end to the era of centralized corporate power—embodied in the attitude that "headquarters knows best"—and a shift to a much more dispersed base of power and influence.

Consider the new patterns of knowledge transfer we are beginning to see. Unilever, for example, is transferring Indian managers with experience in low-cost distribution to China, where they will build a national distribution system and train Chinese managers. And it has transferred Indian managers with knowledge of tier-two markets to Brazil. The phenomenon of using managers from outside the home country to transfer knowledge is relatively new. It will grow over time to the point where the multinational becomes an organization with several centers of expertise and excellence.

Multinationals will be shaped by a wide variety of forces in the coming decades. The big emerging markets will be one of the major forces they come up against. And the effect will be nothing short of dramatic change on both sides. Together, they will challenge each other to change for the better as a truly global twenty-first century economy takes shape. The MNCs will create a higher standard of products, quality, technology, and management practices. Large, opaque markets will gradually become more transparent. The process of transition to market economies will be evolutionary, uneven, and fraught with uncertainties. But the direction is no longer in question.

In order to participate effectively in the big emerging markets, multinationals will increasingly have to reconfigure their resource base, rethink their cost structure, redesign their product development process, and challenge their assumptions about the cultural mix of their top managers. In short, they will have to develop a new mind-set and adopt new business models to achieve global competitiveness in the postimperialist age.

Originally published in July–August 1998
Reprint 98408

Beyond Greening

Strategies for a Sustainable World

STUART L. HART

Executive Summary

THREE DECADES into the environmental revolution, many companies in the industrialized nations have recognized that they can reduce pollution and increase profits at the same time. But beyond corporate "greening" lies the enormous challenge—and opportunity to develop a sustainable global economy, one that the planet is capable of supporting indefinitely.

Stuart Hart, director of the Corporate Environmental Management Program at the University of Michigan School of Business, explains the imperative of sustainable development and provides a framework for identifying the business opportunities behind sustainability. The dangers today are clear: exploding population growth, rapid depletion of resources, and ever more industrialization and urbanization are creating a terrible environmental burden.

121

Companies normally frame greening in terms of risk reduction, reengineering, or cost cutting. But, says Hart, when greening becomes part of strategy, opportunities of potentially staggering proportions open up. A number of companies are moving in that direction. BASF, for example, is colocating plants to make the recycling of waste feasible, and Xerox is reusing parts from leased copiers on new machines.

Hart identifies three stages of environmental strategy: pollution prevention, product stewardship, and the development of clean technology. But companies will not benefit from such efforts unless they draw a road map that can show them how new products and services must evolve and what competencies they will need. Businesses that create a vision of sustainability will be ready to take advantage of the opportunities presented by the need for a sustainable global economy.

THE ENVIRONMENTAL REVOLUTION has been almost three decades in the making, and it has changed forever how companies do business. In the 1960s and 1970s, corporations were in a state of denial regarding their impact on the environment. Then a series of highly visible ecological problems created a groundswell of support for strict government regulation. In the United States, Lake Erie was dead. In Europe, the Rhine was on fire. In Japan, people were dying of mercury poisoning.

Today many companies have accepted their responsibility to do no harm to the environment. Products and production processes are becoming cleaner; and where such change is under way, the environment is on the mend. In the industrialized nations, more and more companies are "going green" as they realize that they can reduce pollution and increase profits simultaneously. We have come a long way.

But the distance we've traveled will seem small when, in 30 years, we look back at the 1990s. Beyond greening lies an enormous challenge—and an enormous opportunity. The challenge is to develop a *sustainable global economy*: an economy that the planet is capable of supporting indefinitely. Although we may be approaching ecological recovery in the developed world, the planet as a whole remains on an unsustainable course. Those who think that sustainability is only a matter of pollution control are missing the bigger picture. Even if all the companies in the developed world were to achieve zero emissions by the year 2000, the earth would still be stressed beyond what biologists refer to as its carrying capacity. Increasingly, the scourges of the late twentieth century—depleted farmland, fisheries, and forests; choking urban pollution; poverty; infectious disease; and migration—are spilling over geopolitical borders. The simple fact is this: in meeting our needs, we are destroying the ability of future generations to meet theirs.

The roots of the problem—explosive population growth and rapid economic development in the emerging economies—are political and social issues that exceed the mandate and the capabilities of any corporation. At the same time, corporations are the only organizations with the resources, the technology, the global reach, and, ultimately, the motivation to achieve sustainability.

It is easy to state the case in the negative: faced with impoverished customers, degraded environments, failing political systems, and unraveling societies, it will be increasingly difficult for corporations to do business. But the positive case is even more powerful. The more we learn about the challenges of sustainability, the clearer it is that we are poised at the threshold of a historic moment in which many of the world's industries may be transformed.

To date, the business logic for greening has been largely operational or technical: bottom-up pollution-prevention programs have saved companies billions of dollars. However, few executives realize that environmental opportunities might actually become a major source of *revenue growth*. Greening has been framed in terms of risk reduction, reengineering, or cost cutting. Rarely is greening linked to strategy or technology development, and as a result, most companies fail to recognize opportunities of potentially staggering proportions.

Worlds in Collision

The achievement of sustainability will mean billions of dollars in products, services, and technologies that barely exist today. Whereas yesterday's businesses were often oblivious to their negative impact on the environment and today's responsible businesses strive for zero impact, tomorrow's businesses must learn to make a positive impact. Increasingly, companies will be selling solutions to the world's environmental problems.

Envisioning tomorrow's businesses, therefore, requires a clear understanding of those problems. To move beyond greening to sustainability, we must first unravel a complex set of global interdependencies. In fact, the global economy is really three different, overlapping economies.

The *market economy* is the familiar world of commerce comprising both the developed nations and the emerging economies.[1] About a billion people—one-sixth of the world's population—live in the developed countries of the market economy. Those affluent societies account for more than 75% of the world's energy and resource consumption and create the bulk of industrial, toxic, and consumer waste. The developed economies thus leave large ecological *footprints*—defined as the amount of land required to meet a typical consumer's needs. (See the exhibit "Ecological Footprints.")

Despite such intense use of energy and materials, however, levels of pollution are relatively low in the developed economies. Three factors account for this seeming paradox: stringent environmental regulations, the greening of industry, and the relocation of the most polluting activities (such as commodity processing and heavy manufacturing) to the emerging market economies. Thus to some extent the greening of the developed world has been at the expense of the environments in emerging economies. Given the much larger population base in those countries, their rapid industri-

---

Ecological Footprints

United States

The Netherlands

India

In the United States, it takes 12.2 acres to supply the average person's basic needs; in the Netherlands, 8 acres; in India, 1 acre. The Dutch ecological footprint covers 15 times the area of the Netherlands, whereas India's footprint exceeds its area by only about 35%. Most strikingly, if the entire world lived like North Americans, it would take three planet Earths to support the present world population.

Source: Donella Meadows, "Our 'Footprints' Are Treading Too Much Earth," Charleston (S.C.) Gazette, April 1, 1996.

alization could easily offset the environmental gains made in the developed economies. Consider, for example, that the emerging economies in Asia and Latin America (and now Eastern Europe and the former Soviet Union) have added nearly 2 billion people to the market economy over the past 40 years.

With economic growth comes urbanization. Today one of every three people in the world lives in a city. By 2025, it will be two out of three. Demographers predict that by that year there will be well over 30 megacities with populations exceeding 8 million and more than 500 cities with populations exceeding 1 million. Urbanization on this scale presents enormous infrastructural and environmental challenges.

Because industrialization has focused initially on commodities and heavy manufacturing, cities in many emerging economies suffer from oppressive levels of pollution. Acid rain is a growing problem, especially in places where coal combustion is unregulated. The World Bank estimates that by 2010 there will be more than 1 billion motor vehicles in the world. Concentrated in cities, they will double current levels of energy use, smog precursors, and emissions of greenhouse gas.

The second economy is the *survival economy*: the traditional, village-based way of life found in the rural parts of most developing countries. It is made up of 3 billion people, mainly Africans, Indians, and Chinese who are subsistence oriented and meet their basic needs directly from nature. Demographers generally agree that the world's population, currently growing by about 90 million people per year, will roughly double over the next 40 years. The developing nations will account for 90% of that growth, and most of it will occur in the survival economy.

Owing in part to the rapid expansion of the market economy, existence in the survival economy is becoming increasingly precarious. Extractive industries and infrastructure development have, in many cases, degraded the ecosystems upon which the survival economy depends. Rural populations are driven further into poverty as they compete for scarce natural resources. Women and children now spend on average four to six hours per day searching for fuelwood and four to six hours per week drawing and carrying water. Ironically, those conditions encourage high fertility rates because, in the short run, children help the family to garner needed resources. But in the long run, population growth in the survival economy only reinforces a vicious cycle of resource depletion and poverty.

Short-term survival pressures often force these rapidly growing rural populations into practices that cause long-term damage to forests, soil, and water. When wood becomes scarce, people burn dung for fuel, one of the greatest—and least well-known—environmental hazards in the world today. Contaminated drinking water is an equally grave problem. The World Health Organization estimates that burning dung and drinking contaminated water together cause 8 million deaths per year.

As it becomes more and more difficult to live off the land, millions of desperate people migrate to already overcrowded cities. In China, for example, an estimated 120 million people now roam from city to city, landless and jobless, driven from their villages by deforestation, soil erosion, floods, or droughts. Worldwide, the number of such "environmental refugees" from the survival economy may be as high as 500 million people, and the figure is growing.

The third economy is *nature's economy*, which consists of the natural systems and resources that support
the market and the survival economies. Nonrenewable
resources, such as oil, metals, and other minerals, are
finite. Renewable resources, such as soils and forests,
will replenish themselves—as long as their use does not
exceed critical thresholds. (See "Aracruz Celulose: A
Strategy for the Survival Economy" at the end of this
article.)

Technological innovations have created substitutes
for many commonly used nonrenewable resources; for
example, optical fiber now replaces copper wire. And in
the developed economies, demand for some virgin materials may actually diminish in the decades ahead
because of reuse and recycling. Ironically, the greatest
threat to sustainable development today is depletion of
the world's *renewable* resources.

Forests, soils, water, and fisheries are all being pushed
beyond their limits by human population growth and
rapid industrial develop-
ment. Insufficient fresh
water may prove to be the
most vexing problem in the
developing world over the
next decade, as agricul-
tural, commercial, and residential uses increase. Water
tables are being drawn down at an alarming rate, especially in the most heavily populated nations, such as
China and India.

*Increasingly, companies
will sell solutions
to the world's
environmental problems.*

Soil is another resource at risk. More than 10% of the
world's topsoil has been seriously eroded. Available
cropland and rangeland are shrinking. Existing crop
varieties are no longer responding to increased use of

fertilizer. As a consequence, per capita world production
of both grain and meat peaked and began to decline
during the 1980s. Meanwhile, the world's 18 major
oceanic fisheries have now reached or actually exceeded
their maximum sustainable yields.

By some estimates, humankind now uses more than
40% of the planet's net primary productivity. If, as projected, the population doubles over the next 40 years, we
may outcompete most other animal species for food,
driving many to extinction. In short, human activity now
exceeds sustainability on a global scale. (See the exhibit
"Major Challenges to Sustainability.")

As we approach the twenty-first century, the interde-
pendence of the three economic spheres is increasingly
evident. In fact, the three economies have become
worlds in collision, creating the major social and environmental challenges facing the planet: climate change,
pollution, resource depletion, poverty, and inequality.

Consider, for example, that the average American
today consumes 17 times more than his or her Mexican
counterpart (emerging economy) and hundreds of times
more than the average Ethiopian (survival economy).
The levels of material and energy consumption in the
United States require large quantities of raw materials
and commodities, sourced increasingly from the survival
economy and produced in emerging economies.

In the survival economy, massive infrastructure
development (for example, dams, irrigation projects,
highways, mining operations, and power generation
projects), often aided by agencies, banks, and corporations in the developed countries, has provided access to
raw materials. Unfortunately, such development has
often had devastating consequences for nature's

Major Challenges to Sustainability

	Pollution	Depletion	Poverty
Developed economies	greenhouse gases use of toxic materials contaminated sites	scarcity of materials insufficient reuse and recycling	urban and minority unemployment
Emerging economies	industrial emissions contaminated water lack of sewage treatment	overexploitation of renewable resources overuse of water for irrigation	migration to cities lack of skilled workers income inequality
Survival economies	dung and wood burning lack of sanitation ecosystem destruction due to development	deforestation overgrazing soil loss	population growth low status of women dislocation

economy and has tended to strengthen existing political and economic elites, with little benefit to those in the survival economy.

At the same time, infrastructure development projects have contributed to a global glut of raw materials and hence to a long-term fall in commodity prices. And as commodity prices have fallen relative to the prices of manufactured goods, the currencies of developing countries have weakened and their terms of trade have become less favorable. Their purchasing power declines while their already substantial debt load becomes even larger. The net effect of this dynamic has been the transfer of vast amounts of wealth (estimated at $40 billion per year since 1985) from developing to developed countries, producing a vicious cycle of resource exploitation and pollution to service mounting debt. Today developing nations have a combined debt of more than $1.2 trillion, equal to nearly half of their collective gross national product.

Strategies for a Sustainable World

Nearly three decades ago, environmentalists such as Paul Ehrlich and Barry Commoner made this simple but powerful observation about sustainable development: the total environmental burden (EB) created by human activity is a function of three factors. They are population (P); affluence (A), which is a proxy for consumption; and technology (T), which is how wealth is created. The product of these three factors determines the total environmental burden. It can be expressed as a formula: $EB = P \times A \times T$.

Achieving sustainability will require stabilizing or reducing the environmental burden. That can be done by decreasing the human population, lowering the level of affluence (consumption), or changing fundamentally the technology used to create wealth. The first option, lowering the human population, does not appear feasible short of draconian political measures or the occurrence of a major public-health crisis that causes mass mortality.

The second option, decreasing the level of affluence, would only make the problem worse, because poverty and population growth go hand in hand: demographers have long known that birth rates are inversely correlated with level of education and standard of living. Thus stabilizing the human population will require improving the education and economic standing of the world's poor, particularly women of childbearing age. That can be accomplished only by creating wealth on a massive scale. Indeed, it may be necessary to grow the world economy as much as tenfold just to provide basic amenities to a population of 8 billion to 10 billion.

That leaves the third option: changing the technology used to create the goods and services that constitute the world's wealth. Although population and consumption may be societal issues, technology is the business of business.

If economic activity must increase tenfold over what it is today just to provide the bare essentials to a population double its current size, then technology will have to improve twentyfold merely to keep the planet at its current levels of environmental burden. Those who believe that ecological disaster will somehow be averted must also appreciate the commercial implications of such a belief: over the next decade or so, sustainable development will constitute one of the biggest opportunities in the history of commerce.

Nevertheless, as of today few companies have incorporated sustainability into their strategic thinking. Instead, environmental strategy consists largely of piecemeal projects aimed at controlling or preventing pollution. Focusing on sustainability requires putting business strategies to a new test. Taking the entire planet as the context in which they do business, companies must ask whether they are part of the solution to social and environmental problems or part of the problem. Only when a company thinks in those terms can it begin to develop a vision of sustainability—a shaping logic that goes beyond today's internal, operational focus on greening to a more external, strategic focus on sustainable development. Such a vision is needed to guide companies through three stages of environmental strategy.

STAGE ONE: POLLUTION PREVENTION

The first step for most companies is to make the shift from pollution control to pollution prevention. Pollution control means cleaning up waste after it has been created. Pollution prevention focuses on minimizing or eliminating waste before it is created. Much like total quality management, pollution prevention strategies depend on continuous improvement efforts to reduce waste and energy use. This transformation is driven by a compelling logic: pollution prevention pays. Emerging global standards for environmental management systems (ISO 14,000, for example) also have created strong incentives for companies to develop such capabilities.

Emerging economies cannot afford to repeat the mistakes of Western development.

Over the past decade, companies have sought to avoid colliding with nature's economy (and incurring the associated added costs) through greening and prevention strategies. Aeroquip Corporation, a $2.5 billion manufacturer of hoses, fittings, and couplings, saw an opportunity here. Like most industrial suppliers, Aeroquip never thought of itself as a provider of environmental solutions. But in 1990, its executives realized that the company's products might be especially valuable in meeting the need to reduce waste and prevent pollution. Aeroquip has generated a $250 million business by focusing its attention on developing products that reduce emissions. As companies in emerging economies realize the competitive benefits of using raw materials and resources more productively, businesses like Aeroquip's will continue to grow.

The emerging economies cannot afford to repeat all the environmental mistakes of Western development. With the sustainability imperative in mind, BASF, the German chemical giant, is helping to design and build chemical industries in China, India, Indonesia, and Malaysia that are less polluting than in the past. By colocating facilities that in the West have been geographically dispersed, BASF is able to create industrial ecosystems in which the waste from one process becomes the raw material for another. Colocation solves a problem common in the West, where recycling waste is often infeasible because transporting it from one site to another is dangerous and costly.

STAGE TWO: PRODUCT STEWARDSHIP

Product stewardship focuses on minimizing not only pollution from manufacturing but also all environmental impacts associated with the full life cycle of a product. As companies in stage one move closer to zero emissions, reducing the use of materials and production of waste requires fundamental changes in underlying product and process design.

Design for environment (DFE), a tool for creating products that are easier to recover, reuse, or recycle, is becoming increasingly important. With DFE, all the effects that a product could have on the environment are examined during its design phase. Cradle-to-grave analysis begins and ends outside the boundaries of a company's operations—it includes a full assessment of all inputs to the product and examines how customers use and dispose of it. DFE thus captures a broad range of external perspectives by including technical staff, environmental experts, end customers, and even community representatives in the process. Dow Chemical Company has pioneered the use of a board-level advisory panel of environmental experts and external representatives to aid its product-stewardship efforts.

By reducing materials and energy consumption, DFE can be highly profitable. Consider Xerox Corporation's Asset Recycle Management (ARM) program, which uses leased Xerox copiers as sources of high-quality, low-cost parts and components for new machines. A well-developed infrastructure for taking back leased copiers combined with a sophisticated remanufacturing process allows parts and components to be reconditioned, tested, and then reassembled into "new" machines. Xerox estimates that ARM savings in raw materials, labor, and waste disposal in 1995 alone were in the $300-million to $400-million range. In taking recycling to this level, Xerox has reconceptualized its business. By redefining the product-in-use as part of the company's asset base, Xerox has discovered a way to add value and lower costs. It can continually provide its lease customers with the latest product upgrades, giving them state-of-the-art functionality with minimal environmental impact.

Product stewardship is thus one way to reduce consumption in the developed economies. It may also aid the quest for sustainability because developing nations often try to emulate what they see happening in the developed nations. Properly executed, product stewardship also offers the potential for revenue growth through product differentiation. For example, Dunlop Tire Corporation and Akzo Nobel recently announced a new radial tire that makes use of an aramid fiber belt rather than the conventional steel belt. The new design makes recycling easier because it eliminates the expensive cryogenic crushing required to separate the steel belts from the tire's other materials. Because the new fiber-belt tire is 30% lighter, it dramatically improves gas mileage. Moreover, it is a safer tire because it improves the traction control of antilock braking systems.

The evolution from pollution prevention to product stewardship is now happening in multinational companies such as Dow, DuPont, Monsanto, Xerox, ABB, Philips, and Sony. For example, as part of a larger sustainability strategy dubbed "A Growing Partnership with Nature," DuPont's agricultural-products business developed a new type of herbicide that has helped farmers around the world reduce their annual use of chemicals by more than 45 million pounds. The new Sulfonylurea herbicides have also led to a 1-billion-pound reduction in the amount of chemical waste produced in the manufacture of agricultural chemicals. These herbicides are effective at 1% to 5% of the application rates of traditional chemicals, are nontoxic to animals and nontarget species, and biodegrade in the soil, leaving virtually no residue on crops. Because they require so much less material in their manufacture, they are also highly profitable.

STAGE THREE: CLEAN TECHNOLOGY

Companies with their eye on the future can begin to plan for and invest in tomorrow's technologies. The simple fact is that the existing technology base in many industries is not environmentally sustainable. The chemical industry, for example, while having made substantial headway over the past decade in pollution prevention and product stewardship, is still limited by its dependence on the chlorine molecule. (Many organochlorides are toxic or persistent or bioaccumulative.) As long as the industry relies on its historical competencies in chlorine chemistry, it will have trouble making major progress toward sustainability.

Monsanto is one company that is consciously developing new competencies. It is shifting the technology base for its agriculture business from bulk chemicals to biotechnology. It is betting that the bioengineering of crops rather than the application of chemical pesticides or fertilizers represents a sustainable path to increased agricultural yields. (See "Growth through Global Sustainability: An Interview with Monsanto's CEO, Robert B. Shapiro," by Joan Magretta, *Harvard Business Review*, January–February 1997.)

Clean technologies are desperately needed in the emerging economies of Asia. Urban pollution there has reached oppressive levels. But precisely because manufacturing growth is so high—capital stock doubles every six years—there is an unprecedented opportunity to replace current product and process technologies with new, cleaner ones.

Japan's Research Institute for Innovative Technology for the Earth is one of several new research and technology consortia focusing on the development and commercialization of clean technologies for the developing world. Having been provided with funding and staff by the Japanese government and more than 40 corporations, RITE has set forth an ambitious 100-year plan to create the next generation of power technology, which will eliminate or neutralize greenhouse gas emissions.

Sustainability Vision

Pollution prevention, product stewardship, and clean technology all move a company toward sustainability. But without a framework to give direction to those activities, their impact will dissipate. A vision of sustainability for an industry or a company is like a road map to the future, showing the way products and services must evolve and what new competencies will be needed to get there. Few companies today have such a road map. Ironically, chemical companies, regarded only a decade ago as the worst environmental villains, are among the few large corporations to have engaged the challenge of sustainable development seriously.

Companies can begin by taking stock of each component of what I call their *sustainability portfolio.* (See the exhibit "The Sustainability Portfolio.") Is there an overarching vision of sustainability that gives direction to the company's activities? To what extent has the company progressed through the three stages of environmental strategy—from pollution prevention to product stewardship to clean technology?

Without a framework for environmental activities, their impact will dissipate.

The Sustainability Portfolio

<table>
<tr>
<td rowspan="2">tomorrow</td>
<td>

Clean technology

Is the environmental performance of our products limited by our existing competency base?

Is there potential to realize major improvements through new technology?

</td>
<td>

Sustainability vision

Does our corporate vision direct us toward the solution of social and environmental problems?

Does our vision guide the development of new technologies, markets, products, and processes?

</td>
</tr>
</table>

<table>
<tr>
<td rowspan="2">today</td>
<td>

Pollution prevention

Where are the most significant waste and emission streams from our current operations?

Can we lower costs and risks by eliminating waste at the source or by using it as useful input?

</td>
<td>

Product stewardship

What are the implications for product design and development if we assume responsibility for a product's entire life cycle?

Can we add value or lower cost while simultaneously reducing the impact of our products?

</td>
</tr>
</table>

internal   external

This simple diagnostic tool can help any company determine whether its strategy is consistent with sustainability. First, assess your company's capability in each of the four quadrants by answering the questions in each box. Then rate yourself on the following scale for each quadrant: 1–nonexistent; 2–emerging; 3–established; or 4–institutionalized. Most companies will be heavily skewed toward the lower left-hand quadrant, reflecting investment in pollution prevention. However, without investments in future technologies and markets (the upper half of the portfolio), the company's environmental strategy will not meet evolving needs.

Unbalanced portfolios spell trouble: a bottom-heavy portfolio suggests a good position today but future vulnerability. A top-heavy portfolio indicates a vision of sustainability without the operational or analytical skills needed to implement it. A portfolio skewed to the left side of the chart indicates a preoccupation with handling the environmental challenge through internal process improvements and technology-development initiatives. Finally, a portfolio skewed to the right side, although highly open and public, runs the risk of being labeled a "greenwash" because the underlying plant operations and core technology still cause significant environmental harm.

Consider the auto industry. During the 1970s, government regulation of tailpipe emissions forced the industry to focus on pollution control. In the 1980s, the industry began to tackle pollution prevention. Initiatives such as the Corporate Average Fuel Efficiency requirement and the Toxic Release Inventory led auto companies to examine their product designs and manufacturing processes in order to improve fuel economy and lower emissions from their plants.

The 1990s are witnessing the first signs of product stewardship. In Germany, the 1990 "take-back" law required auto manufacturers to take responsibility for their vehicles at the end of their useful lives. Innovators such as BMW have influenced the design of new cars with their *design for disassembly* efforts. Industry-level consortia such as the Partnership for a New Generation of Vehicles are driven largely by the product stewardship logic of lowering the environmental impact of automobiles throughout their life cycle.

Early attempts to promote clean technology include such initiatives as California's zero-emission vehicle law and the U.N. Climate Change Convention, which ultimately will limit greenhouse gases on a global scale. But early efforts by industry incumbents have been either incremental—for example, natural-gas vehicles—or defensive in nature. Electric-vehicle programs, for instance, have been used to demonstrate the infeasibility of this technology rather than to lead the industry to a fundamentally cleaner technology.

Although the auto industry has made progress, it falls far short of sustainability. For the vast majority of auto companies, pollution prevention and product stewardship are the end of the road. Most auto executives assume that if they close the loop in both production and design, they will have accomplished all the necessary environmental objectives.

But step back and try to imagine a sustainable vision for the industry. Growth in the emerging markets will generate massive transportation needs in the coming decades. Already the rush is on to stake out positions in China, India, and Latin America. But what form will this opportunity take?

Consider the potential impact of automobiles on China alone. Today there are fewer than 1 million cars on the road in China. However, with a population of more than 1 billion, it would take less than 30% market penetration to equal the current size of the U.S. car market (12 million to 15 million units sold per year). Ultimately, China might demand 50 million or more units annually. Because China's energy and transportation infrastructures are still being defined, there is an opportunity to develop a clean technology yielding important environmental and competitive benefits.

Amory Lovins of the Rocky Mountain Institute has demonstrated the feasibility of building *hypercars*— vehicles that are fully recyclable, 20 times more energy efficient, 100 times cleaner, and cheaper than existing cars. These vehicles retain the safety and performance of conventional cars but achieve radical simplification through the use of lightweight, composite materials, fewer parts, virtual prototyping, regenerative braking, and very small, hybrid engines. Hypercars, which are more akin to computers on wheels than to cars with microchips, may render obsolete most of the competencies associated with today's auto manufacturing—for example, metal stamping, tool and die making, and the internal combustion engine.

Assume for a minute that clean technology like the

hypercar or Mazda's soon-to-be-released hydrogen rotary engine can be developed for a market such as China's. Now try to envision a transportation infrastructure capable of accommodating so many cars. How long will it take before gridlock and traffic jams force the auto industry to a halt? Sustainability will require new transportation solutions for the needs of emerging economies with huge populations. Will the giants in the auto industry be prepared for such radical change, or will they leave the field to new ventures that are not encumbered by the competencies of the past?

A clear and fully integrated environmental strategy should not only guide competency development, it should also shape the company's relationship to customers, suppliers, other companies, policymakers, and all its stakeholders. Companies can and must change the way customers think by creating preferences for products and services consistent with sustainability. Companies must become educators rather than mere marketers of products. (See the exhibit "Building Sustainable Business Strategies.")

For senior executives, embracing the quest for sustainability may well require a leap of faith. Some may feel that the risks associated with investing in unstable and unfamiliar markets outweigh the potential benefits. Others will recognize the power of such a positive mission to galvanize people in their organizations.

Regardless of their opinions on sustainability, executives will not be able to keep their heads in the sand for long. Since 1980, foreign direct investment by multinational corporations has increased from $500 billion to nearly $3 trillion per year. In fact, it now exceeds official development-assistance aid in developing countries.

Building Sustainable Business Strategies

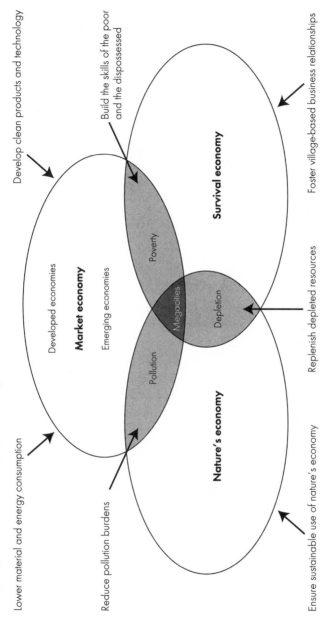

Lower material and energy consumption

Develop clean products and technology

Build the skills of the poor and the dispossessed

Foster village-based business relationships

Developed economies

Market economy

Emerging economies

Survival economy

Poverty

Megacities

Pollution

Depletion

Nature's economy

Reduce pollution burdens

Replenish depleted resources

Ensure sustainable use of nature's economy

With free trade on the rise, the next decade may see the figure increase by another order of magnitude. The challenges presented by emerging markets in Asia and Latin America demand a new way of conceptualizing business opportunities. The rapid growth in emerging economies cannot be sustained in the face of mounting environmental deterioration, poverty, and resource depletion. In the coming decade, companies will be challenged to develop clean technologies and to implement strategies that drastically reduce the environmental burden in the developing world while simultaneously increasing its wealth and standard of living.

Like it or not, the responsibility for ensuring a sustainable world falls largely on the shoulders of the world's enterprises, the economic engines of the future. Clearly, public policy innovations (at both the national and international levels) and changes in individual consumption patterns will be needed to move toward sustainability. But corporations can and should lead the way, helping to shape public policy and driving change in consumers' behavior. In the final analysis, it makes good business sense to pursue strategies for a sustainable world.

Aracruz Celulose: A Strategy for the Survival Economy

"POVERTY IS ONE OF THE WORLD'S leading polluters," notes Erling Lorentzen, founder and chairman of Aracruz Celulose. The $2 billion Brazilian company is the world's largest producer of eucalyptus pulp. "You can't expect people who don't eat a proper meal to be concerned about the environment."[1]

From the very start, Aracruz has been built around a vision of sustainable development. Lorentzen understood that building a viable forest-products business in Brazil's impoverished and deforested state of Espirito Santo would require the simultaneous improvement of nature's economy and the survival economy.

First, to restore nature's economy, the company took advantage of a tax incentive for tree planting in the late 1960s and began buying and reforesting cut-over land. By 1992, the company had acquired over 200,000 hectares and planted 130,000 hectares with managed eucalyptus; the rest was restored as conservation land. By reforesting what had become highly degraded land, unsuitable for agriculture, the company addressed a fundamental environmental problem. At the same time, it created a first-rate source of fiber for its pulping operations. Aracruz's forest practices and its ability to clone seedlings have given the company advantages in both cost and quality.

Aracruz has tackled the problem of poverty head-on. Every year, the company gives away millions of eucalyptus seedlings to local farmers. It is a preemptive strategy, aimed at reducing the farmers' need to deplete the natural forests for fuel or lumber. Aracruz also has a long-term commitment to capability building. In the early years, Aracruz was able to hire local people for very low wages because of their desperate situation. But instead of simply exploiting the abundant supply of cheap labor, the company embarked on an aggressive social-investment strategy, spending $125 million to support the creation of hospitals, schools, housing, and a training center for employees. In fact, until recently, Aracruz spent more on its social investments than it did on wages (about $1.20 for every $1 in wages). Since that time, the standard of living has improved dramatically, as has productivity. The company no longer needs to invest so heavily in social infrastructure.

1. Marguerite Rigoglioso, "Stewards of the Seventh Generation," *Harvard Business School Bulletin*, April 1996, p. 55.

Note

1. The terms *market economy, survival economy,* and *nature's economy* were suggested to me by Vandana Shiva, *Ecology and the Politics of Survival* (New Delhi: United Nations University Press, 1991).

Originally published in January–February 1997
Reprint 97105

Why Focused Strategies May Be Wrong for Emerging Markets

TARUN KHANNA AND KRISHNA PALEPU

Executive Summary

CORE COMPETENCIES AND FOCUS are now the
mantras of corporate strategists in Western economies.
But while managers in the West have dismantled many
conglomerates assembled in the 1960s and 1970s, the
large, diversified business group remains the dominant
form of enterprise throughout many emerging markets.
As those markets open up to global competition, consultants and foreign investors are increasingly pressuring
groups to conform to Western practice by scaling back
the scope of their business activities. Already a number
of executives have decided to break up their groups in
order to show that they are focusing on only a few core
businesses.

There are reasons to worry about this trend, say the
authors. Focus is good advice in New York or London,
but something important gets lost in translation when that

advice is given to groups in emerging markets. Western companies take for granted a range of institutions that support their business activities, but many of those institutions are absent in other regions of the world.

Companies must adapt their strategies to fit their *institutional context:* a country's product, capital, and labor markets; its regulatory system; and its mechanisms for enforcing contracts. In contrast to advanced economies, emerging markets suffer from weak institutions in all or most of these areas. Conglomerates can add value by imitating the functions of several institutions that are present only in advanced economies. Successful groups effectively mediate between their member companies and the rest of the economy.

Core competencies and focus are now the mantras of corporate strategists in Western economies. But while managers in the West have dismantled many conglomerates assembled in the 1960s and 1970s, the large, diversified business group remains the dominant form of enterprise throughout most emerging markets. Some groups operate as holding companies with full ownership in many enterprises, others are collections of publicly traded companies, but all have some degree of central control.

As emerging markets open up to global competition, consultants and foreign investors are increasingly pressuring these groups to conform to Western practice by scaling back the scope of their business activities. The conglomerate is the dinosaur of organizational design, they argue, too unwieldy and slow to compete in today's fast-paced markets. Already a number of executives have decided to break up their groups in order to show that they are focusing on only a few core businesses.

There are reasons to worry about this trend. Focus is good advice in New York or London, but something important gets lost in translation when that advice is given to groups in emerging markets. Western companies take for granted a range of institutions that support their business activities, but many of these institutions are absent in other regions of the world. (See "What Is an Emerging Market?" at the end of this article.) Without effective securities regulation and venture capital firms, for example, focused companies may be unable to raise adequate financing; and without strong educational institutions, they will struggle to hire skilled employees. Communicating with customers is difficult when the local infrastructure is poor, and unpredictable government behavior can stymie any operation. Although a focused strategy may enable a company to perform a few activities well, companies in emerging markets must take responsibility for a wide range of functions in order to do business effectively.

As a result, companies must adapt their strategies to fit their *institutional context*—a country's product, capital, and labor markets; its regulatory system; and its mechanisms for enforcing contracts. Unlike advanced economies, emerging markets suffer from weak institutions in all or most of these areas. (See the table "How Institutional Context Drives Strategy.") It is this difference in institutional context that explains the success of large, diversified corporations in developing economies such as Indonesia and India and their failure in advanced economies such as the United States and the United Kingdom.

How Institutional Context Drives Strategy

Institutional Dimension	United States	Japan	India
Capital market	equity-focused; monitoring by disclosure rules and the market for corporate control	bank-focused; monitoring by interlocking investments and directors	underdeveloped, illiquid equity markets and nationalized banks; weak monitoring by bureaucrats
Labor market	many business schools and consulting firms offering talent; certified skills enhance mobility	few business schools; training internal to companies; company-specific development of talent	few business schools and little training; management talent scarce
Product market	reliable enforcement of liability laws; efficient dissemination of information; many activist consumers	reliable enforcement of liability laws; efficient dissemination of information; some activist consumers	limited enforcement of liability laws; little dissemination of information; few activist consumers
Government regulation	low; relatively free of corruption	moderate; relatively free of corruption	high; corruption common
Contract enforcement	predictable	predictable	unpredictable
Result	**diversified groups have many disadvantages**	**diversified groups have some advantages**	**diversified groups have many advantages**

In our research, we have found that highly diversified business groups can be particularly well suited to the institutional context in most developing countries. From the *chaebols* of Korea to the *business houses* of India to the *grupos* of Latin America, conglomerates can add value by imitating the functions of several institutions that are present only in advanced economies. Successful groups effectively mediate between their member companies and the rest of the economy.

Filling the Institutional Voids

Emerging markets are hardly uniform. Nevertheless, they all fall short to varying degrees in providing the institutions necessary to support basic business operations.

PRODUCT MARKETS

In the case of product markets, buyers and sellers usually suffer from a severe dearth of information for three reasons. First, the communications infrastructure in emerging markets is often underdeveloped. Even as wireless communication spreads throughout the West, vast stretches in countries such as China and India remain without telephones. Power shortages often render the modes of communication that do exist ineffective. The postal service is typically inefficient, slow, or unreliable; and the private sector rarely provides efficient courier services. High rates of illiteracy make it difficult for marketers to communicate effectively with customers.

Second, even when information about products does get around, there are no mechanisms to corroborate the claims made by sellers. Independent consumer-information organizations are rare, and government watchdog agencies are of little use. The few analysts who rate products are generally less sophisticated than their counterparts in advanced economies.

Third, consumers have no redress mechanisms if a product does not deliver on its promise. Law enforcement is often capricious and so slow that few who assign any value to time would resort to it. Unlike in advanced markets, there are few extra-judicial arbitration mechanisms to which one can appeal.

As a result of this lack of information, companies in emerging markets face much higher costs in building credible brands than their counterparts in advanced economies. In turn, established brands wield tremendous power. A conglomerate with a reputation for quality products and services can use its group name to enter new businesses, even if those businesses are completely unrelated to its current lines. Groups also have an advantage when they do try to build up a brand because they can spread the cost of maintaining it across multiple lines of business. Such groups then have a greater incentive not to damage brand quality in any one business because they will pay the price in their other businesses as well.

The Korean chaebols are famous throughout the world for extending their group identity over multiple product categories. Samsung, for example, has used its name for a range of goods from televisions to microwave ovens. Groups in India and Malaysia are beginning to follow suit. The business media in India, for example, abound with advertisements that promote group identity rather than emphasize the products or services of individual companies within a group.

CAPITAL MARKETS

Similar problems occur in capital markets because, without access to information, investors refrain from putting money into unfamiliar ventures. The U.S. capital markets minimize these problems through institutional mechanisms such as reliable financial reporting, a dynamic community of analysts, and an aggressive, independent financial press. Venture capital firms and other intermediaries specialize in investigating and assessing new opportunities. The Securities and Exchange Commission and other watchdog bodies make it difficult for unscrupulous entrepreneurs to mislead unsophisticated investors. As a result, investors have a free flow of largely accurate information about companies. And they can hold corporate managers and directors accountable through the threat of securities litigation, proxy fights, and hostile takeovers. By reducing risks to investors, these institutions make it possible for new enterprises to raise capital on approximately equal terms as big, established companies.

Almost all the institutional mechanisms that make advanced capital markets work so well are either absent or ineffective in emerging markets. Having little information and few safeguards, investors are reluctant to put money into new enterprises. In such a context, diversified groups can point to their track record of returns to investors. As a result, large and well-established companies have superior access to capital markets. This advantage is so pronounced that governments in India and South Korea, for example, have attempted to restrict the amount of credit exposure that banks are permitted to have in large companies.

Conglomerates also can use their internally generated

capital to grow existing businesses or to enter new ones. In fact, their superior ability to raise capital makes groups a prime source of capital for new enterprises and gives them a great advantage over small companies seeking funding. Besides acting as venture capitalists, groups also act as lending institutions to existing member enterprises that are otherwise too small to obtain capital from financial institutions. And some Indian groups, especially those in the automobile sector, have set up subsidiaries whose primary purpose is to provide financing to important suppliers and customers.

At the same time, conglomerates are attractive to foreign investors eager to put money into these often fast-growing markets. With so few financial analysts and knowledgeable mutual-fund managers available to guide them, outsiders instead turn to diversified groups and invest in a wide range of industries. Investors trust groups to evaluate new opportunities and to exercise an auditing and supervisory function. The groups thus become the conduit for large amounts of investment in their capital-starved countries.

LABOR MARKETS

Most emerging markets suffer from a scarcity of well-trained people. While the United States has more than 600 business schools training thousands of future managers every year, Thailand has a handful of high-quality business schools that produce far fewer entry-level managers than the economy needs. Vocational training facilities are also scarce in emerging markets.

Groups can create value by developing promising managers, and they can spread the fixed costs of professional development over the businesses in the group.

Many of the large groups in India, for example, have internal management-development programs—often with dedicated facilities. These programs typically are geared toward developing the skills of experienced managers; but some groups, such as the Malaysian conglomerate Sime Darby, have instituted training programs for all levels of employees in an attempt to develop their human capital. And some of the Korean chaebols have set up special programs in collaboration with top U.S. business schools in order to train their own people.

Groups also can provide much needed flexibility for labor markets in general. Governments in emerging markets usually make it difficult for companies to adjust their workforces to changing economic conditions. Rigid laws often prevent companies from laying off their employees, and labor unions insist on job security in the absence of government-provided unemployment benefits. To counteract the rigidities of the overall labor market, groups can develop extensive internal labor markets of their own. When one company in a group faces declining prospects, its employees can be transferred to other group companies that are on the rise—even to companies in otherwise undesirable locations. India's Aditya Birla group, for example, has acquired a reputation for building communities around its manufacturing plants in the remotest parts of the country. Because the group provides services such as schools, hospitals, and places of worship, managers and other trained employees are more willing to relocate. The growing companies benefit by receiving a ready source of reliable employees.

Groups are also able to put new talent to good use. By allocating talent to where it is most needed, conglomerates have a head start in beginning new activities. The Wipro Group in India successfully moved beyond computers into financial services by relocating skilled engineers first to computer-leasing services that would make use of their technical know-how and then to a broad range of financial services. In contrast, unaffiliated companies usually have to recruit publicly in order to build their operations—a difficult proposition in countries where labor varies widely in quality and lacks certification from respected educational institutions.

REGULATION

As multinational companies know all too well, governments in most emerging markets operate very differently from those in the West. Not only does the state intervene much more extensively in business operations, but companies also have a hard time predicting the actions of regulatory bodies.

Governments in emerging markets are heavily involved in an intricate array of business decisions. Despite the elimination of the old "license raj," for example, Indian law still requires that companies get permission for a range of decisions, such as exiting businesses, changing prices on commodities, and importing raw materials. The law establishes subjective criteria for many of these decisions, so Indian bureaucrats have a great deal of discretion in how they apply the rules.

Diversified groups can add value by acting as intermediaries when their individual companies or foreign partners need to deal with the regulatory bureaucracy. Experience and connections give conglomerates an advantage. The larger the company, the easier it is to carry the cost of maintaining government relationships. Indeed, political economist Dennis Encarnation found that India's large groups maintain "industrial embassies" in New Delhi to facilitate interaction with bureaucrats. Several groups in India also are known for their ability to manage bureaucratic relations at levels all the way down to the village council. India and other countries may be bearing costs for the uncertainty of their regulatory systems. But as long as government officials have so much discretion, companies often end up working with them. Intricate relations between business and government actually appear to be the norm throughout the developing world. The major Malaysian political parties, for example, all have affiliated conglomerates. Until recently, the ties between government and industry in South Korea have been a centerpiece of that country's economic program. Even today in Indonesia, there are groups whose greatest assets appear to include access to high government officials. Because political leaders are so eager to work with companies, managers must be prepared to deal with the government and the bureaucracy.

Not every group adds value in the same way, and no group can hope to fill every institutional void.

Bribes and other corrupt practices may be part of working with the bureaucracy. But that's not the whole story. In many cases, educating officials is more important than exchanging favors. The Enron Corporation, a large U.S.-based multinational, discovered just that when it entered the power generation sector in India. Prepared to invest $2.8 billion, the single largest foreign venture in Indian history, the company had to spend four years and about $20 million educating regulators on the ways international power projects are financed and regulated. Along the way, Enron learned its own lessons about dealing with the Indian bureaucracy and government; the project was almost canceled when Enron's aggressive deal-making style put off newly elected officials in the state where the power plant was to be built. As Enron's executives now acknowledge, experience with Indian politics and bureaucracy might have saved the company a great deal of trouble.

CONTRACT ENFORCEMENT

Despite the extensive involvement of government in emerging markets, these economies lack effective mechanisms to enforce contracts. In advanced economies, companies can work together under arm's-length contractual arrangements because they know the courts will protect them if their partners break their contracts. Confidence in the judicial system makes it easier for everyone to do business. But courts in emerging markets often enforce contracts capriciously or inefficiently; as a result, companies are less likely to be able to resolve disputes through judicial channels.

In such situations, conglomerates can leverage reputations established by honest dealings in the past. Because the misdeeds of one company in a group will damage the prospects of the others, all the group companies have credibility when they promise to honor their agreements with any single partner. They provide a haven where property rights are respected. As a result, suppliers and customers are more willing to work with them.

This credibility pays off the most in relationships with companies seeking to enter emerging markets. Foreign providers of technology or finance need local partners to carry out their strategies, but they worry about being cheated. A reputation for honesty and reliability thus can be a source of enormous competitive advantage. As Alice Amsden and Takashi Hikino have argued, conglomerates in several emerging markets have based much of their success on their ability to access foreign technology. And in India, the largest and most diversified business groups receive a disproportionate share of technology and financial support from advanced economies around the world. The head of RPG Enterprises, India's third largest conglomerate, considers his group's relations with foreign providers—including 16 of the 500 largest U.S. companies—to be among its greatest assets.

Managing the House of Tata

India's largest conglomerate in sales and assets exemplifies how well-run groups can add value in emerging markets. Spanning most sectors of the Indian economy, the Tata companies employ close to 300,000 people and had sales of Rupees 289 billion (U.S. $8.6 billion) in the fiscal year 1995 to 1996. Of the group's 90 companies, more than 40 are publicly traded, and these account for approximately 8% of the total capitalization of the country's publicly traded companies. The companies are all held together by the internationally recognized Tata name and by interlocking investments and directorates.

The Tatas began as a textile mill in 1874, but Indian independence in 1947 brought antimonopoly legislation and high taxes on dividends that encouraged the group to diversify into a variety of unrelated areas. When India began liberalizing its economy in 1991, removing the barriers to growth within any given sector, the group had a stark choice to make. Outside experts advised executives to concentrate on a few strong sectors of

economic activity instead of continuing as an extensively diversified entity. But the executives decided to
remain in most of their existing businesses.

One reason for staying diversified was the difficulty of
exiting businesses because of some remaining legal
restrictions in India as well as the Tatas' reputation as a
benevolent employer. But the Tatas also believed that
they could leverage their size and wide scope to help
their constituent companies in a variety of ways. So they
decided to diversify even further.

Historically, the Tata companies have always come
together to finance the launch of new enterprises. But
initially there was no formal structure for doing so. Then
in 1982, the group created Tata Industries, a venture
capital vehicle funded with a special pool of investment
money drawn from the member companies. Since then,
Tata Industries has sought to lead the Tata group into
information technology, process control, advanced
materials, oil-field services, and other areas. It has provided seed money for several successful ventures, including two computer-manufacturing enterprises—one
cosponsored by Honeywell and another cosponsored by
IBM. Today the Tatas are leading the way in building an
information-technology industrial park in cooperation
with the state of Karnataka and with money and expertise from a consortium that includes the government of
Singapore.

The Tatas were so active in new ventures that by
1995 they needed additional capital. They decided to sell
a stake in Tata Industries at a substantial premium to
Jardine Matheson, itself a diversified company based in
Hong Kong. As a result of the sale, Jardine Matheson
ended up owning 20% of the equity in Tata Industries.
The sale gave the Tatas (and the Indian economy) $200

million in "patient" capital from a conglomerate that shared their long-term approach to investment. Jardine Matheson, in turn, gained exposure to sectors across the Indian economy without having to supervise individual companies.

Many of the group's new ventures benefited from being able to borrow skilled managers from the Tatas' existing businesses. Since 1956, Tata Administrative Services (TAS)—an in-house training program with a national reputation for excellence—has aimed to create a cadre of general managers. Entry into TAS is extremely selective and primarily restricted to graduates of Indian management institutes. Recruits spend their first year on courses, interactive sessions with Tata executives, and visits to major Tata plants around the country. Mentoring and career direction continue for at least five years, as candidates are exposed to three different line functions in three industries to gain a general management perspective.

Fully half of these trainees remain with the Tatas over the long term, in contrast to some other large Indian groups that have to reinvent themselves every few years because of high turnover. For those who do leave, the exit options are attractive, increasing the appeal of joining the Tatas in the first place. In effect, the group provides both management education and a certification service in a country where both are scarce.

TAS consciously organizes its recruits into cohorts according to the year they entered. As recruits spread out to the different companies within the group, they maintain lasting ties with their cohort group, and these networks improve information flows across the group. The head office, mindful of the resources invested in these graduates, encourages group companies to "sacrifice" a talented employee to another company if it is in the interest of both the managers' career development and the group. Cross-company teams of "stars" are assembled to resolve knotty problems that individual companies are having. The group now plans a new initiative, the Tata Group Mobility Plan, to improve the mobility of all skilled managers, including non-TAS graduates, across group companies—and without any loss of benefits.

The Tatas are a favorite of foreign technology providers that are comfortable entering India only with a reputable party. Tata executives consider their reputation for honesty and integrity to be among their greatest assets, and that reputation has led to joint ventures with Daimler-Benz and AT&T, as well as a number of computer companies. Understanding the value of its reputation, the group is developing an internal code of conduct and other elaborate standards regarding the use of the group name. Special fees from the member companies will pay for an internal auditing function to enforce those standards. To foster an orientation toward quality among its companies, Tata also has set up an internal system of awards akin to the United States' Baldrige awards.

By keeping and extending their diversified holdings, the Tatas have maintained a scale and scope that gives them a host of advantages within India's specific institutional context. And these advantage are mutually reinforcing. The more access Tata or any group has to financial capital, the more business opportunities it can offer to talented employees—which in turn helps the group improve quality and enhance its reputation with consumers. Continued success in existing lines of business has made it all the easier for the Tatas to enter new lines of business. The Tatas today have the largest market shares in many sectors of the Indian economy, from steel to computers to hotels.

The Tatas, in turn, benefit the Indian economy. When management consultants told a Tata executive that diversification into unrelated activities did not create value, he replied, "Don't enunciate a theory that will bring everything to a dead halt. If we don't start these businesses, no one else will either, and society will be worse off."

Ensuring That Diversification Adds Value

Once one understands the institutional context of any given emerging market, it is clear why diversified business groups have the potential to add value. (See the table "How Groups Can Add Value.") Nevertheless, groups do not automatically realize that potential. They

How Groups Can Add Value

Institutional Dimension	Institutions That Groups Imitate
Capital market	venture capital firm, private equity provider, mutual fund, bank, auditor
Labor market	management institute/business school, certification agency, head-hunting firm, relocation service
Product market	certification agency, regulatory authority, extrajudicial arbitration service
Government regulation	lobbyist
Contract enforcement	courts, extrajudicial arbitration service

must be actively managed to capture the advantages offered by scale and scope. Our statistical analysis comparing groups and independent companies in India—and a similar analysis on South Korean companies that Tarun Khanna conducted with Yishay Yafeh—suggests that many groups add little or no value to their operations. The largest and most diversified groups, however, do add a good deal of value—perhaps because only these groups have the scale and scope to perform the kind of functions we have described.

Indeed, many groups have actually diminished the value of their member companies through poor management. Conglomerates in emerging markets, after all, suffer from the same problems that plague those in the West: the more activities a business engages in, the harder it is for the head office to coordinate, control, and invest properly in them. Unless a group is ready to offer concrete benefits to its affiliates, companies are better off independent.

Group executives should ask in a systematic way whether they are adding enough value to overcome the costs of complexity and coordination. They should start by assessing their conglomerate's strengths. A group that enjoys brand name recognition in rural markets might think of leveraging its name in unrelated products targeted to the same markets. Or a group that enjoys preferential access to large amounts of capital might consider ventures that require substantial investment.

Of course, not every group will be able to add value in the same way, and no group can hope to fill every institutional void. Decisions to diversify should be based on the group's strengths, not just on growth prospects. Today a number of groups are rushing willy-nilly into power plants and other infrastructure projects all over Asia, and their total-capacity plans already appear to outstrip the likely demand. But there are a few exceptions, such as India's Satyam Group. This group has tried to leverage its reputation for honest and efficient partnerships with foreign companies in order to win the better contracts.

Once a group identifies its opportunities, its executives need to install systems to ensure consistent execution. For example, they must impose discipline over field managers, who will be tempted to take advantage of ready financing to try to build empires. The most successful groups usually have a strong internal auditing system. Sime Darby, the Malaysian conglomerate, benefits from a tradition of strict financial controls and planning that began under its original British managers. Its recent entry into financial services by acquiring UMBC bank was welcomed by the Southeast Asian stock markets, which saw the conglomerate adding value through its management discipline to a large but underperforming company in a rapidly growing sector.

Another strategic imperative for groups is to manage their corporate identities. Given that much of their success depends on the trust of their customers and partners, diversified groups must enforce standards of reliability and quality. The head of Mahindra & Mahindra, a group operating in automobiles and infrastructure in India, grabs every symbolic opportunity he gets to dramatize the importance of never compromising on the product and after-sales service offered to customers.

When a group's strategy depends on supplying functions that are absent in the institutional context, it is important to move with deliberation. Mimicking institutions that are undeveloped in the economy at large requires time and effort. A group that acts as a venture capital firm, for example, needs to develop a track record for nurturing businesses in order to become a magnet for risk capital. It needs to train and retain individuals who are skilled at identifying deals and who can bring their start-up expertise to bear on a variety of situations; it also needs to have disciplined managers to run its high-risk ventures.

Communicating the Strategy to Investors

Even successful conglomerates still face resistance from Western investors and partners who believe that focus is always best. Although many executives may well be tempted to concentrate their operations in order to win favor with outside analysts, a better solution for well-managed groups is to educate investors about the logic underpinning the group's corporate strategy. (See "What Is the Best Institutional Context?" at the end of this article.)

Institutional investors are often most worried not about diversification per se but about the lack of openness in internal group operations. Under the current structure of many conglomerates, investment analysts find it difficult to tell which business segments are creating value within a conglomerate. They fear that a group executive will shuffle funds from one company to another. Faced with these concerns, managers of conglomerates should increase the transparency of their operations, communicate this change to investors, and develop a reputation for doing so.

The Indian group Mahindra & Mahindra is doing just that. While it focuses on automobiles and closely related businesses, the group has set up a holding company to invest in a range of other projects. The automobile company has made a onetime, fully documented infusion of capital to start the holding company so that the group will not have to make repeated transfers of funds for ad-hoc line extensions. If and when the holding company's ventures take off and require new capital, the group will take the company public rather than draw on funds from the automobile company.

If groups are not adding value, they should consider focusing. But they should not break up simply because their competitors are focused foreign companies from advanced economies. Western companies have access to advanced technology, cheap financing, and sophisticated managerial know-how. In the absence of institutions providing these and other functions in emerging markets, diversification may be the best way to match up against the competition.

What is an Emerging Market?

MOST ANALYSTS DEFINE an emerging market according to such characteristics as size, growth rate, or how recently it has opened up to the global economy. In our view, the most important criterion is how well an economy helps buyers and sellers come together. Ideally, every economy would provide a range of institutions in order to facilitate the functioning of markets, but developing countries fall short in a number of ways.

For the purposes of our argument, there are three main sources of market failure:

- **Information Problems.** Buyers—broadly defined not only as consumers in product markets but also as employers in labor markets and investors in financial markets—need reliable information to assess the goods and services that they purchase and the investments that they make. Without adequate information, they are reluctant to do business.

- **Misguided Regulations.** When regulators place political goals over economic efficiency, they can distort the functioning of markets. Many emerging markets, for example, restrict the ability of companies to lay off workers. These rules do add some stability to society—and in some cases, they may even be intended to overcome market failures from other sources. However, the result is that companies are less able to take advantage of opportunities than they are in advanced economies.

- **Inefficient Judicial Systems.** Companies are reluctant to do business without ways of ensuring that their partners will hold up their end of the bargain. Contracts can facilitate cooperation by aligning the incentives of the different parties. Markets therefore depend on judicial systems that are strong enough to enforce contracts in a reliable and predictable way.

In advanced economies, companies can rely on a variety of outside institutions that minimize these sources of market failure. In such a context, companies create value primarily by focusing on a narrow set of activities. At the opposite extreme, stagnant or declining economies usually suffer from near-complete market failure because of the utter absence of basic institutions.

Emerging markets, in the middle of this continuum, offer the prospect of substantial growth because they have developed at least some of the institutions necessary to encourage commerce. But institutional voids are still common enough to cause market failures; as a result, companies in emerging markets often have to perform these basic functions themselves. In our view, that is the crucial distinction between doing business in an emerging market and operating in an advanced economy.

What Is the Best Institutional Context?

EVEN IF THEY ADMIT to the advantages of diversification in emerging markets, some investors or partners may still urge companies to concentrate on a few core activities on the grounds that all markets will eventually develop the West's set of institutions. But their advice assumes that there is one single set of institutions toward which all countries should move. It is unclear, however, whether any one institutional context is obviously superior to others.

Consider the financial system in the United States. That system, based on atomistic shareholders, ensures great liquidity, which generally reduces the cost of funds. Because shareholders can "vote with their feet" if they do not like what management is doing, however, they are less inclined to expend the effort needed to discipline management. As a result, corporate governance may suffer. Similarly, a labor market in which employees freely move from one company to another increases the likelihood that, at any given time, there will be an efficient match between workers' skills and the opportunities to which those skills can be applied. But it reduces the likelihood that workers will invest in anything but the most general skills; as a result, society does not reap the benefits of the long-term, company-specific training of workers.

Japan's institutional context reveals a different resolution to these trade-offs. Japan's capital market is bank centered, not equity centered. Banks monitor managers through equity cross-holdings between companies and board directorships, and the difficulty financial institutions have in unloading their shares encourages them to keep management in line. (Banks, in fact, are at the center of Japan's major *keiretsu*, and these groups offer some of the same advantages of conglomeration that are present in emerging markets.) Japanese managers and workers get their training largely within companies. Managers rarely move around because their expertise is geared toward the specific needs of their company and because they lack credentials from such external institutions as business schools.

Institutional context also takes a long time to evolve. Because different aspects of the institutional environment have often co-evolved into a well-functioning system, changes along any one dimension of an institutional environment can have unanticipated, adverse effects along other dimensions. Economies around the world today are experimenting with moving from one system to another using either "shock therapy" or gradual adjustment—there is much debate about which is the better approach. Deep-seated institutional voids might take decades to be filled. The United States is an extreme example of a country where there are relatively few such voids.

Even if the institutional context of emerging markets evolves to the point that there are no advantages to diversification, executives there should realize that their current opportunities will persist for some time. They are much better served by developing corporate strategies that match their particular contexts instead of blindly applying the management mantra of the day.

Originally published in July–August 1997
Reprint 97404

Competing on Capabilities

The New Rules of Corporate Strategy

GEORGE STALK, PHILIP EVANS, AND
LAWRENCE E. SHULMAN

Executive Summary

IN THE 1980S, COMPANIES DISCOVERED time as a
new source of competitive advantage. In the 1990s,
they will discover that time is only one piece of a more
far-reaching transformation in the logic of competition.
Using examples from Wal-Mart and other highly
successful companies, Stalk, Evans, and Shulman of
the Boston Consulting Group provide managers with
a guide to the new world of "capabilities-based
competition."

In today's dynamic businesses environment, strategy
too must become dynamic. Competition is a "war of
movement" in which success depends on anticipation of
market trends and quick response to changing customer
needs. In such an environment, the essence of strategy is
not the structure of a company's products and markets
but the dynamics of its behavior. To succeed, a com-

171

pany must weave its key business processes into hard-to-imitate strategic capabilities that distinguish it from its competitors in the eyes of customers.

A capability is a set of business processes strategically understood—for example, Wal-Mart's expertise in inventory replenishment, Honda's skill at dealer management, or Banc One's ability to "out-local the national banks and out-national the local banks." Such capabilities are collective and cross-functional—a small part of many people's jobs, not a large part of a few. Finally, competing on capabilities requires strategic investments in support systems that span traditional SBUs and functions and go far beyond what traditional cost-benefit metrics can justify.

A CEO's success in building and managing a company's capabilities will be the chief test of management skill in the 1990s. The prize: companies that combine scale and flexibility to outperform the competition.

In THE 1980s, companies discovered time as a new source of competitive advantage. In the 1990s, they will learn that time is just one piece of a more far-reaching transformation in the logic of competition.

Companies that compete effectively on time—speeding new products to market, manufacturing just in time, or responding promptly to customer complaints—tend to be good at other things as well: for instance, the consistency of their product quality, the acuity of their insight into evolving customer needs, the ability to exploit emerging markets, enter new businesses, or generate new ideas and incorporate them in innovations. But all these qualities are mere reflections of a more fundamental characteristic: a new conception of corporate strategy that we call "capabilities-based competition."

For a glimpse of the new world of capabilities-based competition, consider the astonishing reversal of fortunes represented by Kmart and Wal-Mart.

In 1979, Kmart was king of the discount retailing industry, an industry it had virtually created. With 1,891 stores and average revenues per store of $7.25 million, Kmart enjoyed enormous size advantages. This allowed economies of scale in purchasing, distribution, and marketing that, according to just about any management textbook, are crucial to competitive success in a mature and low-growth industry. By contrast, Wal-Mart was a small niche retailer in the South with only 229 stores and average revenues about half of those of Kmart stores—hardly a serious competitor.

And yet, only ten years later, Wal-Mart had transformed itself and the discount retailing industry. Growing nearly 25% a year, the company achieved the highest sales per square foot, inventory turns, and operating profit of any discount retailer. Its 1989 pretax return on sales was 8%, nearly double that of Kmart. (See the graph "Capabilities Help Wal-Mart Outperform Its Industry.")

Today Wal-Mart is the largest and highest profit retailer in the world—a performance that has translated into a 32% return on equity and a market valuation more than ten times book value. What's more, Wal-Mart's growth has been concentrated in half the United States, leaving ample room for further expansion. If Wal-Mart continues to gain market share at just one-half its historical rate, by 1995 the company will have eliminated all competitors from discount retailing with the exception of Kmart and Target.

Capabilities Help Wal-Mart Outperform Its Industry

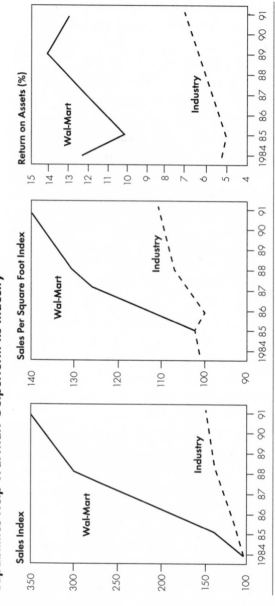

Source: The Boston Consulting Group

The Secret of Wal-Mart's Success

What accounts for Wal-Mart's remarkable success? Most explanations focus on a few familiar and highly visible factors: the genius of founder Sam Walton, who inspires his employees and has molded a culture of service excellence; the "greeters" who welcome customers at the door; the motivational power of allowing employees to own part of the business; the strategy of "everyday low prices" that offers the customer a better deal and saves on merchandising and advertising costs. Economists also point to Wal-Mart's big stores, which offer economies of scale and a wider choice of merchandise.

But such explanations only redefine the question. *Why* is Wal-Mart able to justify building bigger stores? Why does Wal-Mart alone have a cost structure low enough to accommodate everyday low prices and greeters? And what has enabled the company to continue to grow far beyond the direct reach of Sam Walton's magnetic personality? The real secret of Wal-Mart's success lies deeper, in a set of strategic business decisions that transformed the company into a capabilities-based competitor.

The starting point was a relentless focus on satisfying customer needs. Wal-Mart's goals were simple to define but hard to execute: to provide customers access to quality goods, to make these goods available when and where customers want them, to develop a cost structure that enables competitive pricing, and to build and maintain a reputation for absolute trustworthiness. The key to achieving these goals was to make the way the company replenished inventory the centerpiece of its competitive strategy.

This strategic vision reached its fullest expression in a largely invisible logistics technique known as "cross-docking." In this system, goods are continuously delivered to Wal-Mart's warehouses, where they are selected, repacked, and then dispatched to stores, often without ever sitting in inventory. Instead of spending valuable time in the warehouse, goods just cross from one loading dock to another in 48 hours or less.

Cross-docking enables Wal-Mart to achieve the economies that come with purchasing full truck-loads of goods while avoiding the usual inventory and handling costs. Wal-Mart runs a full 85% of its goods through its warehouse system—as opposed to only 50% for Kmart. This reduces Wal-Mart's costs of sales by 2% to 3% compared with the industry average. That cost difference makes possible the everyday low prices.

But that's not all. Low prices in turn mean that Wal-Mart can save even more by eliminating the expense of frequent promotions. Stable prices also make sales more predictable, thus reducing stock-outs and excess inventory. Finally, everyday low prices bring in the customers, which translates into higher sales per retail square foot. These advantages in basic economics make the greeters and the profit sharing easy to afford.

With such obvious benefits, why don't all retailers use cross-docking? The reason: it is extremely difficult to manage. To make cross-docking work, Wal-Mart has had to make strategic investments in a variety of interlocking support systems far beyond what could be justified by conventional ROI criteria.

For example, cross-docking requires continuous contact among Wal-Mart's distribution centers, suppliers, and every point of sale in every store to ensure that orders can flow in and be consolidated and executed within a matter of hours. So Wal-Mart operates a private satellite-communication system that daily sends point-of-sale data directly to Wal-Mart's 4,000 vendors.

Another key component of Wal-Mart's logistics infrastructure is the company's fast and responsive transportation system. The company's 19 distribution centers are serviced by nearly 2,000 company-owned trucks. This dedicated truck fleet permits Wal-Mart to ship goods from warehouse to store in less than 48 hours and to replenish its store shelves twice a week on average. By contrast, the industry norm is once every two weeks.

At Wal-Mart, senior management's job is to help individual store managers learn from the market and from each other.

To gain the full benefits of cross-docking, Wal-Mart has also had to make fundamental changes in its approach to managerial control. Traditionally in the retail industry, decisions about merchandising, pricing, and promotions have been highly centralized and made at the corporate level. Cross-docking, however, turns this command-and-control logic on its head. Instead of the retailer pushing products into the system, customers "pull" products when and where they need them. This approach places a premium on frequent, informal cooperation among stores, distribution centers, and suppliers—with far less centralized control.

The job of senior management at Wal-Mart, then, is not to tell individual store managers what to do but to create an environment where they can learn from the market—and from each other. The company's information systems, for example, provide store managers with detailed information about customer behavior, while a fleet of airplanes regularly ferries store managers to Bentonville, Arkansas headquarters for meetings on market trends and merchandising.

As the company has grown and its stores have multiplied, even Wal-Mart's own private air force hasn't been enough to maintain the necessary contacts a mong store managers. So Wal-Mart has installed a video link connecting all its stores to corporate headquarters and to each other. Store managers frequently hold video-conferences to exchange information on what's happening in the field, like which products are selling and which ones aren't, which promotions work and which don't.

The final piece of this capabilities mosaic is Wal-Mart's human resources system. The company realizes that its frontline employees play a significant role in satisfying customer needs. So it set out to enhance its organizational capability with programs like stock ownership and profit sharing geared toward making its personnel more responsive to customers. Even the way Wal-Mart stores are organized contributes to this goal. Where Kmart has 5 separate merchandise departments in each store, Wal-Mart has 36. This means that training can be more focused and more effective, and employees can be more attuned to customers.

Kmart did not see its business this way. While Wal-Mart was fine-tuning its business processes and organizational practices, Kmart was following the classic textbook approach that had accounted for its original success. Kmart managed its business by focusing on a few product-centered strategic business units, each a profit center under strong centralized line management.

Each SBU made strategy—selecting merchandise, setting prices, and deciding which products to promote. Senior management spent most of its time and resources making line decisions rather than investing in a support infrastructure.

Similarly, Kmart evaluated its competitive advantage at each stage along a value chain and subcontracted activities that managers concluded others could do better. While Wal-Mart was building its ground transportation fleet, Kmart was moving *out* of trucking because a subcontracted fleet was cheaper. While Wal-Mart was building close relationships with its suppliers, Kmart was constantly switching suppliers in search of price improvements. While Wal-Mart was controlling all the departments in its stores, Kmart was leasing out many of its departments to other companies on the theory that it could make more per square foot in rent than through its own efforts.

This is not to say that Kmart managers do not care about their business processes. After all, they have quality programs too. Nor is it that Wal-Mart managers ignore the structural dimension of strategy: they focus on the same consumer segments as Kmart and still have to make traditional strategic decisions like where to open new stores. The difference is that Wal-Mart emphasizes behavior—the organizational practices and business processes in which capabilities rooted—as the primary object of strategy and therefore focuses its managerial attention on the infrastructure that supports capabilities. This subtle distinction has made all the difference between exceptional and average performance. (See the exhibit "Mapping Capabilities: Inventory Replenishment at Wal-Mart.")

Mapping Capabilities: Inventory Replenishment at Wal-Mart

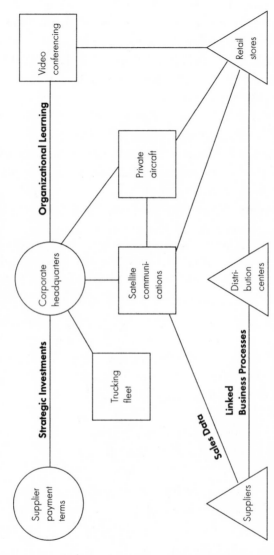

At Wal-Mart, building compatibilities begins with strategic investment: good payment terms to suppliers, a dedicated trucking fleet, satellite communications, company-owned aircraft, and videoconferencing. These investments enable suppliers to respond quickly to sales data beamed directly from stores, distribution centers to deliver new orders in less than 48 hours, and store managers to share best practice. The result: linked business processes that give Wal-Mart its competitive edge.

Four Principles of Capabilities-Based Competition

The story of Kmart and Wal-Mart illustrates the new paradigm of competition in the 1990s. In industry after industry, established competitors are being outmaneuvered and overtaken by more dynamic rivals.

- In the years after World War II, Honda was a modest manufacturer of a 50 cc. engine designed to be attached to a bicycle. Today it is challenging General Motors and Ford for dominance of the global automobile industry.

- Xerox invented xerography and the office copier market. But between 1976 and 1982, Canon introduced more than 90 new models, cutting Xerox's share of the mid-range copier market in half. [1] Today Canon is a key competitor not only in mid-range copiers but also in high-end color copiers.

- The greatest challenge to department store giants like Macy's comes neither from other large department stores nor from small boutiques but from The Limited, a $5.25 billion design, procurement, delivery, and retailing machine that exploits dozens of consumer segments with the agility of many small boutiques.

- Citicorp may still be the largest U.S. bank in terms of assets, but Banc One has consistently enjoyed the highest return on assets in the U.S. banking industry and now enjoys a market capitalization greater than Citicorp's.

These examples represent more than just the triumph of individual companies. They signal a fundamental shift in the logic of competition, a shift that is revolutionizing corporate strategy.

When the economy was relatively static, strategy could afford to be static. In a world characterized by durable products, stable customer needs, well-defined national and regional markets, and clearly identified competitors, competition was a "war of position" in which companies occupied competitive space like squares on a chessboard, building and defending market share in clearly defined product or market segments. The key to competitive advantage was *where* a company chose to compete. *How* it chose to compete was also important but secondary, a matter of execution.

Competition is becoming less like chess and more like an interactive video game.

Few managers need reminding of the changes that have made this traditional approach obsolete. As markets fragment and proliferate, "owning" any particular market segment becomes simultaneously more difficult and less valuable. As product life cycles accelerate, dominating existing product segments becomes less important than being able to create new products and exploit them quickly. Meanwhile, as globalization breaks down barriers between national and regional markets, competitors are multiplying and reducing the value of national market share.

In this more dynamic business environment, strategy has to become correspondingly more dynamic. Competition is now a "war of movement" in which success depends on anticipation of market trends and quick response to changing customer needs. Successful competitors move quickly in and out of products, markets, and sometimes even entire businesses—a process more akin to an interactive video game than to chess. In such an environment, the essence of strategy is *not* the structure of a company's products and markets but the dynamics of its behavior. And the goal is to identify and develop the hard-to-imitate organizational capabilities that distinguish a company from its competitors in the eyes of customers.

Companies like Wal-Mart, Honda, Canon, The Limited, or Banc One have learned this lesson. Their experience and that of other successful companies suggest four basic principles of capabilities-based competition:

1. The building blocks of corporate strategy are not products and markets but business processes.

2. Competitive success depends on transforming a company's key processes into strategic capabilities that consistently provide superior value to the customer.

3. Companies create these capabilities by making strategic investments in a support infrastructure that links together and transcends traditional SBUs and functions.

4. Because capabilities necessarily cross functions, the champion of a capabilities-based strategy is the CEO.

A capability is a set of business processes strategically understood. Every company has business processes that deliver value to the customer. But few think of them as the primary object of strategy. Capabilities-based competitors identify their key business processes, manage them centrally, and invest in them heavily, looking for a long-term payback.

Take the example of cross-docking at Wal-Mart. Cross-docking is not the cheapest or the easiest way to run a warehouse. But seen in the broader context of Wal-Mart's inventory-replenishment capability, it is an essential part of the overall process of keeping retail shelves filled while also minimizing inventory and purchasing in truckload quantities.

What transforms a set of individual business processes like cross-docking into a strategic capability? The key is to connect them to real customer needs. A capability is strategic only when it begins and ends with the customer.

Of course, just about every company these days claims to be "close to the customer." But there is a qualitative difference in the customer focus of capabilities-driven competitors. These companies conceive of the organization as a giant feedback loop that begins with identifying the needs of the customer and ends with satisfying them.

As managers have grasped the importance of time-based competition, for example, they have increasingly focused on the speed of new product development. But as a unit of analysis, new product *development* is too narrow. It is only part of what is necessary to satisfy a customer and, therefore, to build an organizational capability. Better to think in terms of new product *realization*, a capability that includes the way a product is not only developed but also marketed and serviced. The longer and more complex the string of business processes, the harder it is to transform them into a capability—but the greater the value of that capability once built because competitors have more difficulty imitating it.

Weaving business processes together into organizational capabilities in this way also mandates a new logic of vertical integration. At a time when cost pressures are pushing many companies to outsource more and more activities, capabilities-based competitors are integrating vertically to ensure that they, not a supplier or distributor, control the performance of key business processes. Remember Wal-Mart's decision to own its transportation fleet in contrast to Kmart's decision to subcontract.

Even when a company doesn't actually own every link of the capability chain, the capabilities-based competitor works to tie these parts into its own business systems. Consider Wal-Mart's relationships with its suppliers. In order for Wal-Mart's inventory-replenishment capability to work, vendors have to change their own business processes to be more responsive to the Wal-Mart system. In exchange, they get far better payment terms from Wal-Mart than they do from other discount retailers. At Wal-Mart, the average "days payable," the time between the receipt of an invoice from a supplier and its payment, is 29 days. At Kmart, it is 45.

A CEO's success in building capabilities will be the chief test of management skill in the 1990s.

Another attribute of capabilities is that they are collective and cross-functional—a small part of many people's jobs, not a large part of a few. This helps explain why most companies underexploit capabilities-based competition. Because a capability is "everywhere and nowhere," no one executive controls it entirely. Moreover, leveraging capabilities requires a panoply of strategic investments across SBUs and functions far beyond what traditional cost-benefit metrics can justify. Traditional internal accounting and control systems often miss the strategic nature of such investments. For these reasons, building strategic capabilities cannot be treated as an operating matter and left to operating managers, to corporate staff, or still less to SBU heads. It is the primary agenda of the CEO.

Only the CEO can focus the entire company's attention on creating capabilities that serve customers. Only the CEO can identify and authorize the infrastructure investments on which strategic capabilities depend. Only the CEO can insulate individual managers from any short-term penalties to the P&Ls of their operating units that such investments might bring about.

Indeed, a CEO's success in building and managing capabilities will be the chief test of management skill in the 1990s. The prize will be companies that combine scale and flexibility to out perform the competition along five dimensions:

- **Speed.** The ability to respond quickly to customer or market demands and to incorporate new ideas and technologies quickly into products.

- **Consistency.** The ability to produce a product that unfailingly satisfies customers' expectations.

- **Acuity.** The ability to see the competitive environment clearly and thus to anticipate and respond to customers' evolving needs and wants.

- **Agility.** The ability to adapt simultaneously to many different business environments.

- **Innovativeness.** The ability to generate new ideas and to combine existing elements to create new sources of value.

Becoming a Capabilities-Based Competitor

Few companies are fortunate enough to begin as capabilities-based competitors. For most, the challenge is to become one.

The starting point is for senior managers to undergo the fundamental shift in perception that allows them to see their business in terms of strategic capabilities. Then they can begin to identify and link together essential business processes to serve customer needs. Finally, they can reshape the organization—including managerial roles and responsiblities—to encourage the new kind of behavior necessary to make capabilities-based competition work.

The experience of a medical-equipment company we'll call Medequip illustrates this change process. An established competitor, Medequip recently found itself struggling to regain market share it had lost to a new competitor. The rival had introduced a lower priced, lower performance version of the company's most popular product. Medequip had developed a similar product in response, but senior managers were hesitant to launch it.

Their reasoning made perfect sense according to the traditional competitive logic. As managers saw it, the company faced a classic no-win situation. The new product was lower priced but also lower profit. If the company promoted it aggressively to regain market share, overall profitability would suffer.

But when Medequip managers began to investigate their competitive situation more carefully, they stopped defining the problem in terms of static products and markets. Increasingly, they saw it in terms of the organization's business processes.

Traditionally, the company's functions had operated autonomously. Manufacturing was separate from sales, which was separate from field service. What's more, the company managed field service the way most companies do—as a classic profit center whose resources were deployed to reduce costs and maximize profitability. For instance, Medequip assigned full-time service personnel only to those customers who bought enough equipment to justify the additional cost.

However, a closer look at the company's experience with these steady customers led to a fresh insight: at accounts where Medequip had placed one or more full-time service representatives on-site, the company renewed its highly profitable service contracts at three times the rate of its other accounts. When these accounts needed new equipment, they chose Medequip twice as often as other accounts did and tended to buy the broadest mix of Medequip products as well.

The reason was simple. Medequip's on-site service representatives had become expert in the operations of their customers. They knew what equipment mix best suited the customer and what additional equipment the customer needed. So they had teamed up informally with Medequip's salespeople to become part of the selling process. Because the service reps were on-site full-time, they were also able to respond quickly to equipment problems. And of course, whenever a competitor's equipment broke down, the Medequip reps were on hand to point out the product's shortcomings.

This new knowledge about the dynamics of service delivery inspired top managers to rethink how their company should compete. Specifically, they redefined field service from a stand-alone function to one part of an integrated sales and service capability. They crystallized this new approach in three key business decisions.

First, Medequip decided to use its service personnel *not* to keep costs low but to maximize the life-cycle profitability of a set of targeted accounts. This decision took the form of a dramatic commitment to place at least one service rep on-site with selected customers— no matter how little business each account currently represented.

The decision to guarantee on-site service was expensive, so choosing which customers to target was crucial; there had to be potential for considerable additional business. The company divided its accounts into three categories: those it dominated, those where a single competitor dominated, and those where several competitors were present. Medequip protected the accounts it dominated by maintaining the already high level of service and by offering attractive terms for renewing service contracts. The company ignored those customers dominated by a single competitor—unless the competitor was having serious problems. All the remaining resources were focused on those accounts where no single competitor had the upper hand.

Next Medequip combined its sales, service, and order-entry organizations into cross-functional teams that concentrated almost exclusively on the needs of the targeted accounts. The company trained service reps in sales techniques so they could take full responsibility for generating new sales leads. This freed up the sales staff to focus on the more strategic role of understanding the long-term needs of the customer's business. Finally, to emphasize Medequip's new commitment to total service, the company even taught its service reps how to fix competitors' equipment.

Once this new organizational structure was in place, Medequip finally introduced its new low-price product. The result: the company has not only stopped its decline in market share but also *increased* share by almost 50%. The addition of the lower priced product has reduced profit margins, but the overall mix still includes many higher priced products. And absolute profits are much higher than before.

This story suggests four steps by which any company can transform itself into a capabilities-based competitor:

Shift the strategic framework to achieve aggressive goals. At Medequip, managers transformed what looked like a no-win situation—either lose share or lose profits—into an opportunity for a major competitive victory. They did so by abandoning the company's traditional function, cost, and profit-center orientation and by identifying and managing the capabilities that link customer need to customer satisfaction. The chief expression of this new capabilities-based strategy was the decision to provide on-site service reps to targeted accounts and to create cross-functional sales and service teams.

Organize around the chosen capability and make sure employees have the necessary skills and resources to achieve it. Having set this ambitious competitive goal, Medequip managers next set about reshaping the company in terms of it. Rather than retaining the existing functional structure and trying to encourage coordination through some kind of matrix, they created a brand new organization—Customer Sales and Service—and divided it into "cells" with overall responsibility for specific customers. The company also provided the necessary training so that employees could understand how their new roles would help achieve new business goals. Finally, Medequip created systems to support employees in their new roles. For example, one information system uses CD-ROMs to give field-service personnel quick access to information about Medequip's product line as well as those of competitors.

Make progress visible and bring measurements and reward into alignment. Medequip also made sure that the company's measurement and reward systems reflected the new competitive strategy. Like most companies, the company had never known the profitability of individual customers. Traditionally, field-service employees were measured on overall service profitability. With the shift to the new approach, however, the company had to develop a whole new set of measures—for example, Medequip's "share-by-customer-by-product," the amount of money the company invested in servicing a particular customer, and the customer's current and estimated lifetime profitability. Team members' compensation was calculated according to these new measures.

Do not delegate the leadership of the transformation. Becoming a capabilities-based competitor requires an enormous amount of change. For that reason, it is a process extremely difficult to delegate. Because capabilities are cross-functional, the change process can't be left to middle managers. It requires the hands-on guidance of the CEO and the active involvement of top line managers. At Medequip, the heads of sales, service, and order entry led the subteams that made the actual recommendations, but it was the CEO who oversaw the change process, evaluated their proposals, and made the final decision. His leading role ensured senior management's commitment to the recommended changes.

This top-down change process has the paradoxical result of driving business decision making down to those directly participating in key processes—for example, Medequip's sales and service staff. This leads to a high measure of operational flexibility and an almost reflex-like responsiveness to external change.

A New Logic of Growth: The Capabilities Predator

Once managers reshape the company in terms of its underlying capabilities, they can use these capabilities to define a growth path for the corporation. At the center of capabilities-based competition is a new logic of growth.

In the 1960s, most managers assumed that when growth in a company's basic business slowed, the company should turn to diversification. This was the age of the multibusiness conglomerate. In the 1970s and 1980s, however, it became clear that growth through diversification was difficult. And so, the pendulum of management thinking swung once again. Companies were urged to "stick to their knitting"—that is, to focus on their core business, identify where the profit was, and get rid of everything else. The idea of the corporation became increasingly narrow.

Competing on capabilities provides a way for companies to gain the benefits of both focus and diversification. Put another way, a company that focuses on its strategic capabilities can compete in a remarkable diversity of regions, products, and businesses and do it far more coherently than the typical conglomerate can. Such a company is a "capabilities predator"—able to come out of nowhere and move rapidly from nonparticipant to major player and even to industry leader.

Capabilities-based companies grow by transferring their essential business processes—first to new geographic areas and then to new businesses. Wal-Mart CEO David Glass alludes to this method of growth when he characterizes Wal-Mart as "always pushing the inside out; we never jump and backfill."

Strategic advantages built on capabilities are easier to transfer geographically than more traditional competitive advantages. Honda, for example, has become a manufacturer in Europe and the United States with relatively few problems. The quality of its cars made in the United States is so good that the company is exporting some of them back to Japan.

In many respects, Wal-Mart's move from small towns in the South to large, urban, northern cities spans as great a cultural gap as Honda's move beyond Japan. And yet, Wal-Mart has done it with barely a hiccup. While the stores are much bigger and the product lines different, the capabilities are exactly the same. Wal-Mart simply replicates its system as soon as the required people are trained. The company estimates that it can train enough new employees to grow about 25% a year.

But the big payoff for capabilities-led growth comes not through geographical expansion but through rapid entry into whole new businesses. Capabilities-based companies do this in at least two ways. The first is by "cloning" their key business processes. Again, Honda is a typical example.

Most people attribute Honda's success to the innovative design of its products or the way the company manufactures them. These factors are certainly important. But the company's growth has been spearheaded by less visible capabilities.

For example, a big part of Honda's original success in motorcycles was due to the company's distinctive capability in "dealer management," which departed from the traditional relationship between motorcycle manufacturers and dealers. Typically, local dealers were motorcycle enthusiasts who were more concerned with finding a way to support their hobby than with building a strong business. They were not particularly interested in marketing, parts-inventory management, or other business systems.

The key to Honda's growth from motorcycles to lawn mowers and automobiles is the way the company manages its dealer relationships.

Honda, by contrast, managed its dealers to ensure that they would become successful businesspeople. The company provided operating procedures and policies for merchandising, selling, floor planning, and service management. It trained all its dealers and their entire staffs in these new management systems and supported them with a computerized dealer-management information system. The part-time dealers of competitors were no match for the better prepared and better financed Honda dealers.

Honda's move into new businesses, including lawn mowers, outboard motors, and automobiles, has depended on re-creating this same dealer-management capability in each new sector. Even in segments like luxury cars, where local dealers are generally more service-oriented than those in the motorcycle business, Honda's skill at managing its dealers is from transforming service standards. Honda dealers consistently receive the highest ratings for customer satisfaction among auto companies selling in the United States. One reason is that Honda gives its dealers far more autonomy to decide on the spot whether a needed repair is covered by warranty. (See "How Capabilities Differ from Core Competencies: The Case of Honda." at the end of this article.)

But the ultimate form of growth in the capabilities-based company may not be cloning business processes so much as creating processes so flexible and robust that the same set can serve many different businesses. This is the case with Wal-Mart. The company uses the same inventory-replenishment system that makes its discount stores so successful to propel itself into new and traditionally distinct retail sectors.

Take the example of warehouse clubs, no-frills stores that sell products in bulk at a deep discount. In 1983, Wal-Mart created Sam's Club to compete with industry founder Price Club and Kmart's own PACE Membership Warehouse. Within four years, Sam's Club sales had passed those of both Price and PACE, making it the largest wholesale club in the country. Sam's 1990 sales were $5.3 billion, compared with $4.9 billion for Price and $1.6 billion for PACE. What's more, Wal-Mart has repeated this rapid penetration strategy in other retail sectors, including pharmacies, European-style hyper-markets, and large, no-frills grocery stores known as superstores. (See the graph "Portrait of a Capabilities Predator.")

Portrait of a Capabilities Predator

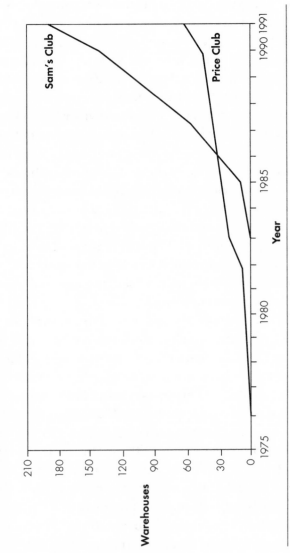

By applying capabilities developed in its core business, Wal-Mart was able to penetrate the wholesale club market quickly. Its unit, Sam's Club, overtook industry leader Price Club in a mere four years.
Source: The Boston Consulting Group

While Wal-Mart has been growing by quickly entering these new businesses, Kmart has tried to grow by acquisition, with mixed success. In the past decade, Kmart has bought and sold a number of companies in unrelated businesses such as restaurants and insurance—an indication the company has had difficulty adding value.

This is not to suggest that growth by acquisition is necessarily doomed to failure. Indeed, the company that is focused on its capabilities is often better able to target sensible acquisitions and then integrate them successfully. For example, Wal-Mart has recently begun to supplement its growth "from the inside out" by acquiring companies—for example, other small warehouse clubs and a retail and grocery distributor—whose operations can be folded into the Wal-Mart system.

It is interesting to speculate where Wal-Mart will strike next. The company's inventory-replenishment capability could prove to be a strong competitive advantage in a wide variety of retail businesses. In the past decade, Wal-Mart came out of nowhere to challenge Kmart. In the next decade, companies such as Toys "R" Us (Wal-Mart already controls as much as 10% of the $13 billion toy market) and Circuit City (consumer electronics) may find themselves in the sights of this capabilities predator.

The Future of Capabilities-Based Competition

For the moment, capabilities-based companies have the advantage of competing against rivals still locked into the old way of seeing the competitive environment. But such a situation won't last forever. As more and more

companies make the transition to capabilities-based
competition, the simple fact of competing on capabilities will become less important than the specific capabilities a company has chosen to build. Given the necessary
long-term investments, the strategic choices managers
make will end up determining a company's fate.

If Wal-Mart and Kmart are a good example of the present state of capabilities-based competition, the story of
two fast-growing regional banks suggests its future.
Wachovia Corporation, with dual headquarters in
Winston-Salem, North Carolina and Atlanta, Georgia, has
superior returns and growing market share throughout its
core markets in both states. Banc One, based in Colum-
bus, Ohio, has consistently enjoyed the highest return on
assets in the U.S. banking industry. Both banks compete
on capabilities, but they do it in very different ways.

Wachovia competes on its ability to understand and
serve the needs of individual customers, a skill that
manifests itself in probably the highest "cross-sell
ratio"—the average number of products per customer—
of any bank in the country. The linchpin of this capability is the company's roughly 600 "personal bankers,"
frontline employees who provide Wachovia's mass-
market customers with a degree of personalized service
approaching what has traditionally been available only
to private banking clients. The company's specialized
support systems allow each personal banker to serve
about 1,200 customers. Among those systems: an integrated customer-information file, simplified work processes that allow the bank to respond to almost all customer requests by the end of business that day, and a
five-year personal banker training program.

Where Wachovia focuses on meeting the needs of
individual customers, Banc One's distinctive ability is to

understand and respond to the needs of entire *communities*. To do community banking effectively, a bank has to have deep roots in the local community. But traditionally, local banks have not been able to muster the professional expertise, state-of-the-art products, and highly competitive cost structure of large national banks like Citicorp. Banc One competes by offering its customers the best of both these worlds. Or in the words of one company slogan, Banc One "out-locals the national banks and out-nationals the local banks."

Striking this balance depends on two factors. One is local autonomy. The central organizational role in the Banc One business system is played not by frontline employees but by the presidents of the 51 affiliate banks in the Banc One network. Affiliate presidents have exceptional power within their own region. They select products, establish prices and marketing strategy, make credit decisions, and set internal management policies. They can even over-rule the activities of Banc One's centralized direct-marketing businesses. But while Banc One's affiliate system is highly decentralized, its success also depends on an elaborate, and highly centralized, process of continuous organizational learning. Affiliate presidents have the authority to mold bank products and services to local conditions, but they are also expected to learn from best practice throughout the Banc One system and to adapt it to their own operations.

Banc One collects an extraordinary amount of detailed and current information on each affiliate bank's internal and external performance. For example, the bank regularly publishes "league tables" on numerous measures of operating performance, with the worst performers listed first. This encourages collaboration to improve the weakest affiliates rather than competition to be the best. The bank also continuously engages in workflow re-engineering and process simplification. The 100 most successful projects, known as the "Best of the Best," are documented and circulated among affiliates.

Wachovia and Banc One both compete on capabilities. Both banks focus on key business processes and place critical decision-making authority with the people directly responsible for them. Both manage these processes through a support system that spans the traditional functional structure, and senior managers concentrate on managing this system rather than controlling decisions. Both are decentralized but focused, single-minded but flexible.

But there the similarities end. Wachovia responds to individual customers en masse with personalization akin to that of a private banker. Banc One responds to local markets en masse with the flexibility and canniness of the traditional community bank. As a result, they

Capabilities are often mutually exclusive; choosing the right ones is the essence of strategy.

focus on different business processes: Wachovia on the transfer of customer-specific information across numerous points of customer contact; Banc One on the transfer of best practices across affiliate banks. They also empower different levels in the organization: the personal banker at Wachovia, the affiliate president at Banc One.

Most important, they grow differently. Because so much of Wachovia's capability is embedded in the training of the personal bankers, the bank has made few acquisitions and can integrate them only very slowly. Banc One's capabilities, by contrast, are especially easy to transfer to new acquisitions. All the company needs to do is install its corporate MIS and intensively train the acquired bank's senior officers, a process that can be done in a few months, as opposed to the much longer period it takes Wachovia to train a new cadre of front-line bankers. Banc One has therefore made acquisitions almost a separate line of business.

If Banc One and Wachovia were to compete against each other, it is not clear who would win. Each would have strengths that the other could not match. Wachovia's capability to serve individual customers by cross-selling a wide range of banking products will in the long term probably allow the company to extract more profit per customer than Banc One. On the other hand, Wachovia cannot adapt its products, pricing, and promotion to local market conditions the way Banc One can. And Wachovia's growth rate is limited by the amount of time it takes to train new personal bankers.

Moreover, these differences are deep-seated. They define each of the two companies in ways that are not easy to change. Capabilities are often mutually exclusive. Choosing the right ones is the essence of strategy.

How Capabilities Differ from Core Competencies: The Case of Honda

IN THEIR INFLUENTIAL 1990 *Harvard Business Review* article, "The Core Competence of the Corporation," Gary Hamel and C.K. Prahalad mount an attack on traditional notions of strategy that is not so dissimilar from what we are arguing here. For Hamel and Prahalad, however, the central building block of corporate strategy is "core competence." How is a competence different from a capability, and how do the two concepts relate to each other?

Hamel and Prahalad define core competence as the combination of individual technologies and production skills that underlie a company's myriad product lines. Sony's core competence in miniaturization, for example, allows the company to make everything from the Sony Walkman to videocameras to notebook computers. Canon's core competencies in optics, imaging, and microprocessor controls have enabled it to enter markets as seemingly diverse as copiers, laser printers, cameras, and image scanners.

As the above examples suggest, Hamel and Prahalad use core competence to explain the ease with which successful competitors are able to enter new and seemingly unrelated businesses. But a closer look reveals that competencies are not the whole story.

Consider Honda's move from motorcycles into other businesses, including lawn mowers, outboard motors, and automobiles. Hamel and Prahalad attribute Honda's success to its underlying competence in engines and power trains. While Honda's engine competence is certainly important, it alone cannot explain the speed with which the company has successfully moved into a wide range of businesses over the past 20 years. After all, General Motors (to take just one example) is also an accomplished designer and manufacturer of engines. What distinguishes Honda from its competitors is its focus on capabilities.

One important but largely invisible capability is Honda's expertise in "dealer management"—its ability to train and support its dealer network with operating procedures and policies for merchandising, selling, floor planning, and service management. First developed for its motorcycle business, this set of business processes has since been replicated in each new business the company has entered.

Another capability central to Honda's success has been its skill at "product realization." Traditional product development separates planning, proving, and executing into three sequential activities: assessing the market's needs and whether existing products are meeting those needs; testing the proposed product; then building a prototype. The end result of this process is a new factory or organization to introduce the new product. This traditional approach takes a long time—and with time goes money.

Honda has arranged these activities differently. First, planning and proving go on continuously and in parallel. Second, these activities are clearly separated from execution. At Honda, the highly disciplined execution cycle schedules major product revisions every four years and minor revisions every two years. The 1990 Honda Accord, for example, which is the first major redesign of that model since 1986, incorporates a power train developed two years earlier and first used in the 1988 Accord. Finally, when a new product is ready, it is released to *existing* factories and organizations, which dramatically shortens the amount of time needed to launch it. As time is reduced, so are cost and risk.

Consider the following comparison between Honda and GM. In 1984, Honda launched its Acura division; one year later, GM created Saturn. Honda chose to integrate Acura into its existing organization and facilities. In Europe, for example, the Acura Legend is sold through the same sales force as the Honda Legend. The Acura division now makes three models—the Legend, Integra, and Vigor—and is turning out 300,000 cars a year. At the end of 1991, seven years after it was launched, the division had produced a total of 800,000 vehicles. More important, it had already introduced eight variations of its product line.

By contrast, GM created a separate organization and a separate facility for Saturn. Production began in late 1990, and 1991 will be its first full model year. If GM is lucky, it will be producing 240,000 vehicles in the next year or two and will have two models out.

As the Honda example suggests, competencies and capabilities represent two different but complementary dimensions of an emerging paradigm for corporate strategy. Both concepts emphasize "behavioral" aspects of strategy in contrast to the traditional structural model. But whereas core competence emphasizes technological and production expertise at specific points along the value chain, capabilities are more broadly based, encompassing the entire value chain. In this respect, capabilities are visible to the customer in a way that core competencies rarely are.

Like the "grand unified theory" that modern-day physicists are searching for to explain physical behavior at both the subatomic level and that of the entire cosmos, the combination of core competence and capabilities may define the universal model for corporate strategy in the 1990s and beyond.

Note

1. See T. Michael Nevens, Gregory L. Summe, and Bro Uttal, "Commercializing Technology: What the Best Companies Do," *Harvard Business Review*, May–June 1990, p. 154.

Originally published in March–April 1992
Reprint 92209

Corporate Strategy

The Quest for Parenting Advantage

ANDREW CAMPBELL, MICHAEL GOOLD, AND
MARCUS ALEXANDER

Executive Summary

WHILE THE CORE COMPETENCE CONCEPT appealed
powerfully to companies disillusioned with diversification,
it did not offer any practical guidelines for developing
corporate-level strategy. To fill the gap, the authors propose the parenting framework, with tools for answering
two questions: Which business should a company own?
What parenting approach will get the best performance
from those businesses?

Instead of looking at how businesses relate to one
another, a parent organization should look at how well
its skills fit its businesses' needs and whether owning
them creates or destroys value. Businesses that seem
related, such as minerals and oil, often require completely different skills.

To determine the fit between a parent and its businesses, corporate strategists should look at four areas:

the critical success factors of the business, the parenting opportunities in the business, the characteristics of the parents, and the financial results. Next, to determine which businesses to keep and which to divest, they should rank them into five categories: those that clearly fit well; those that fit in some ways bbut not in others; those that fit comfortably but have little potential for further value creation; those with a possibility of value destruction; and those that fit in parenting opportunities but not in critical success factors.

Changing the portfolio to fit the parent organization is usually easier than trying to change the parent to fit its businesses. That is why demergers and breakups have been on the increase.

The best multibusiness companies do more than simply create value. They strive to create more value than rivals would. They are on a quest for parenting advantage.

As THEY CRAFT CORPORATE-LEVEL STRATEGY, most chief executives today fail to address two crucial questions: What businesses should this company, rather than rival companies, own and why? And what organizational structure, management processes, and philosophy will foster superior performance from its businesses?

We are not saying that chief executives intentionally avoid or ignore those questions. They simply lack the tools and processes for the job. Most planning processes focus on developing business-level, rather than corporate-level, strategies. Even more important, the planning frameworks that corporate-level strategists have commonly used have proven inappropriate or impractical.

The growth/share matrix, introduced in the 1970s and adopted by two-thirds of all U.S. corporations within a decade, encouraged companies to balance their business portfolios with a mix of stars, cash cows, and question marks. But the poor performance of companies using the portfolio-management technique, and disillusionment with diversification, have discouraged all but a handful of companies from using it today.

For the past five to ten years, increasing numbers of companies have been trying to stick to their knitting, as Tom Peters and Bob Waterman first advised in their book *In Search of Excellence* in 1982. Companies have been shedding the businesses they acquired as diversifications in order to focus instead on core businesses, relying for guidance on the core competence concept. In introducing the concept ("The Core Competence of the Corporation," *Harvard Business Review,* May–June 1990), C.K. Hamel and Gary Prahalad proposed that companies should build portfolios of businesses around shared technical or operating competencies and should develop structures and processes to enhance their core competencies.

Despite its powerful appeal, the core competence concept has not provided practical guidelines for developing corporate-level strategy. Many companies have tried to define their core competencies, but, lacking reliable analytical tools, few have achieved the clarity they sought. Furthermore, the core competence model does not account for the success of companies such as ABB Asea Brown Boveri, BTR, Emerson Electric, General Electric, Hanson, and Kohlberg Kravis

The best parent companies create more value in their businesses than rivals would.

Roberts, whose businesses have limited technical or operating overlap.

The framework we propose—the parenting framework—fills in the deficiencies of the core competence concept. It provides a rigorous conceptual model as well as the tools needed for an effective corporate-level planning process.

Based on research with some of the world's most successful diversified companies, the parenting framework is grounded in the economics of competitive strategy. Multibusiness companies bring together under a parent organization businesses that could potentially be independent. Such parent companies can justify themselves economically only if their influence creates value. For example, the parent organization can improve the businesses' plans and budgets, promote better linkages among them, provide especially competent central functions, or make wise choices in its own acquisitions, divestments, and new ventures.

Multibusiness companies create value by influencing—or parenting—the businesses they own. The best parent companies create more value than any of their rivals would if they owned the same businesses. Those companies have what we call *parenting advantage.*

Previous strategic frameworks have focused on the businesses in the portfolio and searched for a logic by examining how they relate to one another. The underlying assumption has been that portfolios of related businesses perform better than portfolios of unrelated ones. The growth/share matrix implies that businesses are related if their cash, profit, and growth performance create a balance within the portfolio. The core competence concept says that businesses are related if they have common technical or operating know-how. The parenting framework, in contrast, focuses on the competencies of the parent organization and on the value created from the relationship between the parent and its businesses. The parent organization is an intermediary between investors and businesses. It competes not only with other parent organizations but also with other intermediaries, such as investment trusts and mutual funds. Corporate-level strategies, therefore, make sense to the extent that the parent creates sufficient value to compete with other intermediaries. That occurs when the parent's skills and resources fit well with the needs and opportunities of the businesses. If there is a fit, the parent is likely to create value. If there is not a fit, the parent is likely to destroy value. The parent, we have found, is highly influential, and its impact is rarely neutral.

Demerger decisions, such as the one facing Imperial Chemical Industries (ICI) in 1992, dramatically illustrate the importance of fit between the parent and its businesses. To split a large and venerable organization that had been built up over decades demanded a powerful rationale. (See "Why ICI Chose to Demerge," *Harvard Business Review*, March–April 1995.)

Divestment decisions, such as the exit of oil companies from the minerals business, also illustrate the logic of the fit. Companies such as British Petroleum (BP), Exxon, and Shell entered minerals in order to diversify. They believed they had the appropriate skills for that business because, like oil, it involved exploration, extraction, government relations, and large, technically complex projects. Minerals and oil seemed to share competencies.

However, after more than ten years of experience, oil companies are getting out of the minerals business. BP sold its minerals businesses to the RTZ Corporation in

1989, and Shell recently sold its operations to Gencor in South Africa. Why? Because their minerals businesses have consistently under-performed those of minerals specialists. The minerals businesses of Atlantic Rich-field, BP, Exxon, Shell, and Standard Oil had an average pretax return on sales of −17% during the mid-1980s, while independent metal companies achieved a 10% return. One reason for the disparity is the influ-ence that managers in oil-company parents exercised over decisions made in their metals businesses. As a man-ager in BP's minerals businesses explains, "The problem was that the BP managing directors could not really come to grips with the minerals business or feel they understood it. There was always that vestige of suspi-cion that led to a temptation to say no to proposals from the business or, alternatively, if they said yes, to say yes for the wrong reasons." In other words, the influence of the parent managers on the minerals business was faulty because of insufficient understanding—an insufficient fit—between the parent and the business.

Fit between a parent and its businesses is a two-edged sword: a good fit can create value; a bad one can destroy it.

   The oil companies' diversification into minerals failed because, despite similarities, some success factors in minerals are different from those in oil. Exploration, for instance, is not as critical. Finding new mineral deposits is not necessarily a passport to profit. More important is access to low-cost deposits because only those deposits make profits in cyclical downturns. For minerals busi-nesses, forming joint ventures with companies that already have low-cost mines can be more profitable than searching for new deposits. Pressure from oil-company managers to spend more on exploration was therefore counter-productive. RTZ, the new parent of BP's minerals businesses, has not had that problem, however. "It has been easy to add value," Robert Adams, RTZ's planning director, explains, "because we have some specialist expertise in mine planning and operations and a natural affinity for the investment and exploration decisions and trade-offs that you face in cyclical minerals businesses."

The oil-company examples show that fit between parent and businesses is a two-edged sword. A good fit can create additional value; a bad one can destroy value. Bad parenting causes business-unit managers to make worse decisions than they would otherwise. In one company, the managers in the minerals business had taken bad advice about exploration techniques from their oil-company bosses. When asked why, they replied, "They had acquired us so we thought they must know something we didn't."

Our framework for developing corporate-level strategy is based on assessing the nature of the fit between the corporate parent and its businesses. Is there a match that will create value, or a mismatch that will destroy value? By answering that question, corporate strategists can consider which changes—either to the portfolio of businesses or to the parenting approach—will improve fit.

Assessing Fit

Few corporate-level managers find it easy to assess the fit between the corporate parent and its businesses. The reason, in part, is that they seldom openly address the question. But even if they do, it is a tough question to answer. It is like asking whether a particular manager fits a particular job. One must understand a great deal about the manager and the job to judge well.

To aid those judgments, we have developed a structured analytical approach. It begins with an assessment of the businesses. First, we examine the critical success factors of each business. We need to understand those factors in order to judge where the parent's influence is positive and where it is negative. Second, we document areas in the businesses in which performance can be improved. Those are areas in which the parent can add value. They represent the upside potential.

Armed with those analyses, we then review the characteristics of the parent, grouped in a number of categories. That analysis ensures that managers will consider all the main characteristics of the parent when they judge whether its influence is likely to fit the business's opportunities and needs. The final step is to test the judgments against the results that the businesses achieve under the influence of the parent.

Whether a parent and its businesses fit is a tough question that few managers address.

CRITICAL SUCCESS FACTORS: UNDERSTANDING THE BUSINESSES

The concept of critical success factors is familiar to most managers. In every business, certain activities or issues are critical to performance and to the creation of competitive advantage. However, success factors differ among and even within industries. For example, those in bulk chemicals are not the same as those in specialty chemicals.

Most business-level plans define the critical success factors as part of the rationale for the actions proposed. A special analysis of critical success factors is not, therefore, usually necessary to develop corporate-level strategy. However, it is a good idea to summarize critical success factors, confirm their importance with business-level managers, and check whether circumstances in the business have changed—for example, whether its costs have risen. (See the table "Critical Success Factors for a Diversified Food Company.")

Critical-success-factor analysis is an important base for assessing fit. It is useful in judging whether friction is likely to develop between the business and the parent. A parent that does not understand the critical success factors in a business is likely to destroy value. It is also useful for judging how similar the parenting needs of different businesses are. In the food-company example, the restaurant and retail businesses are more similar than the hotel, property, and food-products businesses. Finally, critical-success-factor analysis is a prerequisite for a parenting-opportunity analysis.

PARENTING OPPORTUNITIES: GAUGING THE UPSIDE

To add value, a parent must improve its businesses. For that to be possible, there must be room for improvement. We call the potential for improvement within a business a *parenting opportunity*.

Many kinds of parenting opportunities may present themselves. For example, a business may have excessive overhead costs that its managers are unaware of. For the right parent, the high overhead is an opportunity. Or two businesses might be able to gain economies of scale by combining their sales forces. The businesses' managers may find such consolidation difficult because of personal animosities or loyalties, or concerns about control. The combining of sales forces is, therefore, an

Critical Success Factors for a Diversified Food Company

Success Factors	Food products	Property	Restaurant A	Restaurant B	Retail	Hotels
Product branding	●					●
Selling	●					●
Product mix management	●					
Scale and capacity utilization	●					
Business development skills		●				
Formula branding			●	●	●	
Positioning to match locality		●	●	○	●	
Site selection		●	○	●	●	●
Property development costs		●	○	●		●
Value engineering			●	●		○
Detailed operating controls			●	●	●	●
Management selection and training			●	●	●	●
Supply chain logistics	●		●	●	●	●
Low overheads	●	●	●	●	●	●

opportunity for the right parent. In another example, a business may have good, but not world-class, manufacturing and logistics management skills. A parent company that has world-class expertise in those areas can help that business. (See "Ten Places to Look for Parenting Opportunities," at the end of this article, for a checklist of circumstances in which parenting opportunities can arise.)

Most businesses have parenting opportunities and could improve their performance if they had a parent organization with exactly the right skills and experience. The purpose of a parenting-opportunity analysis is to document those opportunities and estimate their significance. The analysis can be a major challenge, though, because the parent often needs a depth of expertise in the business to identify the opportunities. For example, a parent that is not expert in manufacturing might not know that a business lacked world-class manufacturing skills. Or a parent without detailed knowledge of a business's market may not be aware of the opportunity to combine sales forces.

Three types of analyses can help strategists identify parenting opportunities. First, strategists list the major challenges facing a business, which are normally recorded in the business plan. Then they examine each challenge to see whether it contains a parenting opportunity. For example, one business faced two major challenges: to expand capacity in order to meet the demands of a growing segment and to lower costs by improving purchasing. The first challenge did not contain a parenting opportunity, because the business-unit managers had already successfully expanded capacity many times and would likely be able to do so again without parenting influence. However, the second challenge did contain a parenting opportunity: the business-unit managers had weak purchasing skills and had never recruited a top-ranking purchasing manager. A parent with suitable skills would be able to coach the business managers, helping them avoid pitfalls, such as offering a salary too low to attract someone with the expertise they need.

In the second type of analysis, strategists document the most important influences the parent has on the business and then judge whether those influences are addressing parenting opportunities that were not identified in the first analysis. For example, at one parent company, the central engineering function develops the technical procedures and standards for all its chemical businesses. Conversations with business-unit and central-engineering managers confirmed that having a central department develop standards addressed a parenting opportunity. The business-unit managers lacked the skills and time to become expert in technical and engineering standards. Moreover, the businesses were sufficiently similar so that technical lessons learned in one situation could be applied to others. Central engineering was able to create value by helping the businesses raise technical standards.

A third kind of analysis looks at the influence different parent companies have on similar businesses to see whether they have discovered still other parenting opportunities. This step requires that managers learn about rival parent companies through public documents, individuals in those companies, or consultants and industry observers. Frequently, rivals share information about their parenting activities, believing it to be of low commercial value.

CHARACTERISTICS OF THE PARENT: ASSESSING FIT

The next step in developing a corporate-level strategy is to decide how closely the parent organization fits with the businesses in the portfolio. That involves documenting the characteristics of the parent organization, then comparing them with the critical success factors and parenting opportunities in each of the businesses.

Parenting characteristics fall into five categories:

• the mental maps that guide parent managers;

• the corporate structure, management systems, and processes;

• the central functions, services, and resources;

• the nature, experience, and skills of managers in the parent organization; and

• the extent to which companies have decentralized by delegating responsibilities and authority to business-unit managers.

The five categories are lenses through which one can view the influences of the parent. Although the categories have obvious links and overlaps, analyzing each one separately ensures a comprehensive understanding of the parent. (See "Understanding the Parent," at the end of this article, for a fuller description of the categories.)

With a good grasp of a parent's characteristics and hence of the influence it exercises, strategists can then ask two key questions:

• Does the parent have characteristics—that is, the skills, resources, management processes, and so

forth—that fit the parenting opportunities in the
business? Can the parent exploit the upside potential
of the relationship?

- Is there a misfit between the parent's characteristics
  and the business's critical success factors? What is
  the potential downside of the relationship?

The 1989 acquisition of Champion International Corporation, the spark-plug company, by Texas-based manufacturer Cooper Industries illustrates the importance of
the two questions. Cooper uses a distinctive parenting
approach designed to help its businesses raise their
manufacturing performance. New acquisitions are
"Cooperized"—Cooper audits their manufacturing operations; improves their cost accounting systems; makes
their planning, budgeting, and human resource systems
conform with its systems; and centralizes union negotiations. One business manager observes, "When you are
acquired by Cooper, one of the first things that happens
is a truckload of policy manuals arrives at your door."
Such hands-on parenting has been effective in transforming the cost and quality of certain kinds of manufacturing businesses.

The issue facing Cooper was whether Champion
would fit with that parenting approach. For example,
would Cooper's manufacturing-services department be
able to add value to Champion? Manufacturing at
Champion fell short of best practice, offering a major
opportunity for Cooper's parenting skills. But there were
some worries. Spark plugs involve ceramic manufacturing, an area about which Cooper's manufacturing-
services department knew little. Moreover, Champion's
factories produced millions of spark plugs annually in
high-volume processes, while Cooper's manufacturing

staff was most knowledgeable about slower, cell-based or batch-process operations. In addition, Champion had a number of operations outside the United States, while Cooper had less experience working in foreign countries.

To judge Champion's fit, Robert Cizik, Cooper's CEO, had to examine his company's parenting characteristics and assess the potential and risks for each one. What would be the impact of centralizing union negotiations, imposing Cooper's cost accounting processes, and so on? Cizik had to judge the net effect of all those influences.

In addition, he had to consider whether Cooper's parenting influence would be better for Champion than that of rivals. Dana Corporation, another manufacturing-oriented parent company, also spotted the opportunity at Champion. Would Cooper's impact on Champion be greater than Dana's and hence justify the premium Cooper had to pay to acquire the business in direct competition with Dana?

IMPACT ON RESULTS: VALIDATING THE JUDGMENTS

One can test a company's judgments about how well its parenting characteristics fit with its businesses by examining the company's track record with different sorts of businesses. A technique we call *success and failure analysis* is a useful way of summarizing a parent's track record. The analysis involves listing important decisions and classifying each as a success, a failure, or neutral. It is often useful to group decisions by type: for example, key appointments, major capital investments, new product launches, or acquisitions. By identifying the influences of the parent and by searching for patterns of success and failure, one can identify types of situations in which the parent's influence is positive or negative. (See the graph "Success and Failure Analysis.")

Performance analysis is yet another way of validating managers' judgments about fit. It involves reviewing the performance of each business in comparison with its competitors. Businesses with comparatively poor results

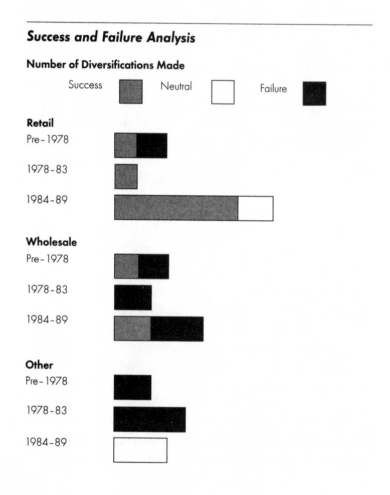

Success and Failure Analysis

Number of Diversifications Made

Success   Neutral   Failure

Retail
Pre-1978

1978-83

1984-89

Wholesale
Pre-1978

1978-83

1984-89

Other
Pre-1978

1978-83

1984-89

are probably not benefiting from, and may be hobbled by, the parent's influence. However, strategists must exercise care in reaching such conclusions. A business may be performing well or poorly without the parent having any significant influence on it. One must be sure that the performance is due to the parent's influence before using such evidence to assess fit. The real question is whether the business is performing better or worse than it would as a stand-alone, independent company. One way to make that judgment is to compare the performance of different businesses in a company's portfolio with their par return on investment, as predicted by the Profit Impact of Market Strategies (PIMS) methodology. PIMS is a research database of detailed information on thousands of business units, submitted by participating companies. One of the uses of the database is to provide par performance statistics for a business, based on responses to a questionnaire about its structural and strategic characteristics.

Profitability that is much higher or lower than par levels is a strong indication that the parent has had an impact. However, even then, strategists must understand to what extent the unusual performance is due to the influence of the parent.

The Fit Assessment at BTR

BTR, one of Great Britain's most successful companies, illustrates the importance of the fit between a parent and its businesses. In the industrial manufacturing businesses that make up the bulk of BTR's portfolio, the company's characteristics fit well both with the parenting opportunities that the company is targeting and with its businesses' critical success factors. BTR has gone from strength to strength, often achieving margins on sales in the 15% to 20% range, while competitors settle for 5% to 10%.

Sir Owen Green, managing director of BTR from 1967 to 1987, identified certain parenting opportunities in industrial manufacturing businesses. Particularly in mature niche areas, he found that businesses often underperform. Their financial information on product profitability may not tell them where they are making money and where they need to improve productivity. Their fear of losing customers may cause them to underprice, especially with larger customers. They may adopt a fill-the-factory mentality and pursue marginal sales, particularly in a recession. In an attempt to move away from mature product areas, they often diversify in a way that is wasteful.

Green learned from experience that BTR could improve those businesses' performance dramatically. For instance, by imposing a more rigorous budgeting and financial-reporting system, he encouraged business managers to pinpoint their richest profit sources, cut unnecessary costs, and achieve higher productivity. By pushing for price increases in line with or ahead of inflation, he showed managers how they could get higher prices from good customers. By focusing managers' attention on margins rather than sales, he helped managers shed the fill-the-factory mentality. By insisting on a tight business definition focused around the skills of the factory, he dissuaded managers from diversifying wastefully.

Over the years, BTR has developed parenting characteristics that fit its businesses, as described in "Understanding the Parent" at the end of this article. Green's insights, his commitment to giving managers responsibility for meeting profit targets, and his understanding of the critical success factors in industrial manufacturing businesses are now written into the *mental maps* that guide BTR's parenting.

BTR's *structure* comprises a large number of small, tightly defined, autonomous profit centers, each with its own management team. The company's renowned profit-planning *process,* which demands detailed cost and profit information for every product line in every business, shapes its management systems. The process permits parent managers to challenge and stretch the profit targets of the businesses, to press for price increases and margin improvements, and to raise the standards of financial management

The words on the boardroom clock epitomize BTR's culture: "Think of rest and work on."

throughout the company. The profit-planning process has become a powerful tool in the hands of the BTR parent managers, who have accumulated vast experience in interpreting the plans and comparing the performance of many similar profit centers.

BTR does not believe in large *central staffs* or *functional resources.* As Alan Jackson, BTR's current CEO, explains, "It is very important to remember that each business remains separate. We certainly do not have any nonsense like central marketing or group marketing directors. We do not blunt the edges of clear business-unit focus. That would be criminal." Corporate headquarters is small and concentrates mainly on financial control, with only 60 employees in London and similarly small groups in the corporate offices in the United States and Australia. The headquarters building is modest, and its furnishings seem to have changed little since it was built in the 1960s. The inscription on the board-room clock epitomizes the company's culture: "Think of rest and work on."

The primary *skills* of the people in the parent organization involve motivating and controlling profit center managers and using the profit-planning process to improve their performance. Nearly all the BTR senior managers have long personal experience with industrial manufacturing businesses.

Finally, the *decentralization contract* gives profit center managers the freedom to make their own decisions, as long as their profit-planning ratios and bottom line are satisfactory. The parent interferes in running its businesses only when it sees ways to enhance performance.

"Our game is really in industrial manufacturing," Jackson comments. "We know how to set up a plant. We know how to get productivity improvements. We know how to downsize and squeeze when volumes fall." In such businesses, BTR is good both at seeing the parenting opportunities and at understanding the critical success factors.

BTR's approach, however, fitted less well with some of the distribution businesses it obtained as part of larger acquisitions. That is not because there are no parenting opportunities to be found in cost reduction, productivity improvement, or pricing, which are BTR's forte. Rather, distribution businesses have some critical success factors that do not fit BTR's approach.

A structured analysis cannot replace judgment. Managers must be honest about their own strengths and weaknesses.

"We have found that it is much harder to downsize distribution businesses when volumes fall," Jackson explains. The BTR approach seeks to maintain margins even when volumes decline, which is often possible in industrial manufacturing because true fixed costs are a small percentage of the total. In some distribution businesses, the approach does not work because of the relatively high fixed costs associated with maintaining a distribution network. "As volumes fall," Jackson says, "we press for cost reductions, and that can be achieved only by closing depots. But closing depots causes further volume losses and weakens the rest of the network."

The financial results also indicate a poor fit between the parent and its businesses. BTR's distribution businesses have not outperformed competitors in the same way that its manufacturing businesses typically do. In manufacturing, BTR's return on sales is frequently double that of the average competitor, while margins in distribution are closer to industry norms. "We have been less successful away from industrial manufacturing," Jackson says. "Distribution businesses need a different sort of philosophy." So he decided to divest some of BTR's distribution businesses, such as National Tyre Service in Great Britain and Texas-based Summers Group. The parenting opportunities in distribution businesses were not great enough to warrant a change in BTR's parenting approach.

The BTR example shows that fit assessments require difficult judgments about the parent's positive and negative influences. A structured analytical approach to making those judgments can help by breaking the problem into smaller elements and ensuring that analysts take all relevant aspects of the parent and the businesses into account. But analysis cannot replace judgment. Parent managers must be honest with themselves about their own strengths and weaknesses. Most companies will find they have a good fit with some portfolio businesses and a poor one with others. The challenge for the corporate strategist is to decide which changes in parenting are appropriate.

Making Changes to Improve Fit

To pull the judgments about fit together and rank a company's businesses, it helps to summarize the assessments into a matrix. (See the graph "Parenting-Fit Matrix for a Diversified Food Company.")

The horizontal axis of the matrix records how well the parent's characteristics fit the business's parenting

Parenting-Fit Matrix for a Diversified Food Company

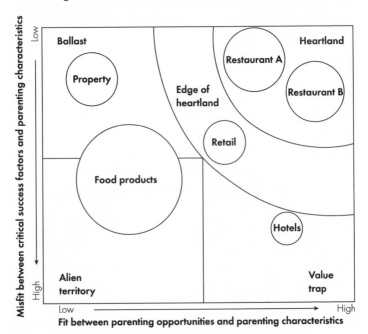

Fit between parenting opportunities and parenting characteristics

opportunities—the first set of judgments made in the fit assessment. The vertical axis records the extent of any misfit between the parent's characteristics and the business's critical success factors—the second set of judgments made in the fit assessment. A good fit reduces the danger of destroying value in a business.

Each portfolio business can be located on the matrix. The matrix in our illustration plots the businesses of the diversified food company described in the table of critical success factors. Each position on the matrix has implications for the company's corporate strategy.

HEARTLAND BUSINESSES

Businesses that fall in the top right corner should be at the heart of the company's future. Heartland businesses have opportunities to improve that the parent knows how to address, and they have critical success factors the parent understands well.

In the case of the two restaurant businesses in the graph, the parent provides high-quality services in property development, food purchasing, menu management, and staff scheduling. The parent also has skills in formula branding, in setting performance targets that generate above-average restaurant margins, and in designing flat structures for chain operations that keep overheads per unit to a minimum. Furthermore, the parent does not have any characteristics that will destroy value; none of its characteristics conflict with the businesses' critical success factors.

Heartland businesses should have priority in the company's portfolio development, and the parenting characteristics that fit its heartland businesses should form the core of the parent organization.

EDGE-OF-HEARTLAND BUSINESSES

For some businesses, making clear judgments is difficult. Some parenting characteristics fit; others do not. We call those businesses, such as the retail business in the food-company example, *edge of heartland*. The parent's skills in staff scheduling, brand management, and lean organizational structures appear to add value to the business. However, the added value is partly offset by critical success factors that fit less well with the parent. For example, the retail business requires skills in site selection and property development that are different from those required for the restaurants. The parent's influence in those areas is probably negative. With edge-of-heartland businesses, the parent both creates and destroys value. The net contribution is not clear-cut. Such businesses are likely to consume much of the parent's attention, as it tries to clarify its judgments about them and, if possible, transform them into heartland businesses.

Many edge-of-heartland businesses move into the heartland when the parent learns enough about the critical success factors to avoid destroying value. Sometimes that means changing the parent's behavior or the business's strategy, but often the solution is for the parent to learn when not to intervene and when to be sensitive to special pleas from the business.

When Unilever acquired Calvin Klein's perfume business, it adjusted its usual parenting approach to increase the potential for value creation. For instance, Unilever did not impose its famous human resource management processes on Calvin Klein, because it recognized that its managers and Calvin Klein's would not mix easily. Unilever also did not impose its marketing policies, which would have conflicted with Calvin Klein's. Calvin

Klein, for instance, does not use market research to launch its upmarket perfumes in the same way Unilever does to launch mass-market products. Unilever treated Calvin Klein as a global business, while its own personal-products businesses are national or regional. To accommodate the differences between Calvin Klein and its other businesses, Unilever changed or neutralized many of its usual parenting influences and channeled most contact between the two companies through a single person.

BALLAST BUSINESSES

Most portfolios contain a number of *ballast businesses,* in which the potential for further value creation is low but the business fits comfortably with the parenting approach. That situation often occurs when the parent understands the business extremely well because it has owned it for many years or because some of the parent managers previously worked in it. The parent may have added value in the past but can find no further parenting opportunities. In the food-company example, the property business fits that category. The business owns a large number of sites that are leased to third parties. The company has little potential for adding value to the business operation because it has identified no parenting opportunities. It also has little potential for destroying value because the parent managers are so familiar with the property-business issues.

Most managers instinctively choose to hold on to familiar businesses. Sometimes that is the right decision, but it should always be examined. Ballast businesses can be important sources of stability, providing steady cash flow and reliable earnings. But ballast businesses can also be a drag on the company, slowing growth in value creation and distracting parent managers from more productive activities. Moreover, there is a danger that changes in the business environment can turn ballast businesses into what we call *alien territory.*

Managers should search their ballast businesses for new parenting opportunities that might move them into heartland or edge-of-heartland territory. If that effort fails or if the parenting opportunities that are discovered fit better with a rival's characteristics, companies should divest the ballast business as soon as they can get a price that exceeds the expected value of future cash flows. Not surprisingly, that advice is difficult for most managers to take. Profitable businesses requiring little parent attention seem ideal. However, the risks of holding on to them may be substantial. Companies with too many ballast businesses can easily become targets for a takeover.

ALIEN-TERRITORY BUSINESSES

Most corporate portfolios contain at least a smattering of businesses in which the parent sees little potential for value creation and some possibility of value destruction. Those businesses are alien territory for that parent. Frequently, they are small and few in a portfolio—the remnants of past experiments with diversifications, pet projects of senior managers, businesses acquired as part of a larger purchase, or attempts to find new growth opportunities. But, in the food-company example, the largest business—food products—fits partly into alien territory, even though it is the company's original core business. The industry has become international, so the national business has become less competitive. The parent's

managers have little international experience and have
mostly come up through the restaurant side of the company. Their influence is more likely to destroy than to
create value in the business.

Managers normally concede that alien-territory businesses do not fit with the company's parenting approach
and would perform better with another parent. Nevertheless, parent managers often have reasons for not
divesting them: the business is currently profitable or in
the process of a turnaround; the business has growth
potential, and the parent is learning how to improve the
fit; there are few ready buyers; the parent has made
commitments to the business's managers; the business
is a special favorite of the chairman; and so forth. The
reality, however, is that the relationship between
such businesses and the parent organization is likely to
be destroying value. They should be divested sooner
rather than later. The company in our example should
sell its food-products business to an international food
company.

Companies need to be clear about their heartland
before they can recognize alien territory. They also need
to be clear about their alien territory in order to recognize their heartland. Hence, as companies describe their
heartland businesses, they will give as many negative criteria—which are alien-territory criteria—as they do positive ones. For example, here is how managers at Cooper
Industries describe their heartland: manufacturing businesses, metal-based manufacturing in particular rather
than service or assembly; businesses with proprietary
products and strong technology; cell-based manufacturing, not continuous process; businesses whose marketing and distribution costs are less than manufacturing
costs; businesses with strong market positions; busi-

nesses large enough to support Cooper's overhead; and businesses with no intractable environmental or union problems. The criteria help Cooper strategists sort among heartland, edge-of-heartland, and alien-territory businesses and improve their acquisition and divestment decisions. Cooper has exited a number of businesses that did not fit its criteria. Most recently, it proposed divesting its original business—oil tools.

VALUE-TRAP BUSINESSES

Parent managers make their biggest mistakes with *value-trap businesses.* They are businesses with a fit in parenting opportunities but a misfit in critical success factors. The potential for upside gain often blinds managers to the misfit—that is, downside risks.

In the food-company example, the hotel business is a value trap. The parent believed its restaurant and retail skills would bring success in the hotel business. Management initially saw it as an edge-of-heartland experiment, with parenting opportunities in food purchasing, property-development costs, and performance benchmarking. But value was destroyed in

Managers make their biggest mistakes with businesses that fit in parenting opportunities but not in critical success factors.

other vital areas. Hotel businesses require selling skills, referrals from other businesses, and specialized site selection. The parent's influence in those areas proved highly negative, and, five years after its acquisition, the business is probably worth half the capital invested in it.

The logic of core competence can push parent managers into value traps as they strive for growth through diversification. In Europe, many privatized utility companies have created engineering consultancies and construction companies on the basis of their competence in engineering and managing large construction projects. But the parent organizations' bureaucratic policies, planning systems, and decision processes, which are geared to their capital-intensive base businesses, proved to be severe disadvantages for the new businesses. The parents burdened their businesses with unreasonable overheads, restrained them from paying appropriate salaries, encouraged them to overspend on balance-sheet items, and prevented them from grasping market opportunities in a timely manner. What sounded like a synergistic core competence has led the parents into a value trap.

Changing Parenting Characteristics

Faced with a spread of businesses across the parenting-fit matrix, as in the graph, managers might assume that they should change the skills and resources of the parent organization in order to move all their businesses into the top right corner. Our research suggests, however, that parenting characteristics are built on deeply held values and beliefs, making changes hard to implement. Good parents constantly modify and fine-tune their parenting, but fundamental changes in parenting seldom occur, usually only when

While good parents are always fine-tuning their parenting, they rarely change in fundamental ways.

the chief executive and senior-management team are replaced.

It is also difficult for parent organizations to behave in fundamentally different ways toward different businesses in their portfolios. The interlocking nature of parenting characteristics, pressures for fair and equal treatment of all businesses, and deeply held attitudes all mean that a parent tends to exert similar influences on all its businesses. Alan Jackson's recognition of the difficulties likely to arise from treating BTR's distribution and manufacturing businesses differently persuaded him to sell the distribution businesses rather than compromise the corporate philosophy.

Companies are coming to understand that it is often easier to change the portfolio to fit the parent organization than to change the parent organization to fit the businesses. That realization accounts for the rise in demergers and corporate-level breakups. ICI, for example, chose to divide into two portfolios rather than attempt to be a good parent to businesses with widely different parenting needs.

THE PROCESS WE HAVE DESCRIBED is a structured means of creating corporate-level strategy. Critical-success-factor analysis identifies areas in which the parent's influence is inappropriate. Parenting-opportunity analysis focuses attention on the upside potential. The parenting-fit matrix ranks the businesses, exposing those with lower levels of fit.

The most immediate benefit that companies receive from such analyses is identifying misfits. With that knowledge, they start to reduce the impact of bad parenting techniques and exit alien-territory businesses.

Additional value creation comes from focusing on the best parenting opportunities and developing the parenting skills to match. But it is a long-term challenge requiring the parent to learn new skills. Moreover, maintaining fit is a dynamic process. As the needs of the businesses change, the parent organization must continually review its behavior and its portfolio of businesses.

Companies without sound corporate-level strategies gradually lose strength and fall prey to hostile predators or become emaciated from periodic downsizing and cost cutting. Excessive overhead consumes profits, businesses that do not fit lose ground to competitors, and decisions are guided by the wrong criteria. Management fads, cash availability, or business-level performance—rather than parenting fit—influence acquisition decisions. Bureaucratic tidiness, arbitrary cost targets, or organizational politics—rather than value creation—influence changes in the parent.

Companies with sound corporate-level strategies create value from a close fit between the parent's skills and the businesses' needs. The best companies, however, do more. They strive to be the best parents for the businesses they own—to create more value than rivals would. They are on a quest for parenting advantage.

Just as the concept of competitive advantage has been one of the greatest contributors to clearer thinking about business-level strategy, we believe the concept of parenting advantage can achieve the same for corporate-level strategy. Parenting advantage not only drives planning; it also helps executives make decisions. Will an acquisition, divestment, corporate function, coordination committee, reporting relationship, or planning process enhance parenting advantage? If not, it should be reexamined and new ideas generated.

Ten Places to Look for Parenting Opportunities

Size and Age. Old, large, successful businesses often accumulate bureaucracies and overheads that are hard to eliminate from the inside. Small, young businesses may have insufficient functional skills, managerial-succession problems, and insufficient financial resources to ride out a recession. Are those factors relevant to the business?

Management. Does the business employ top-quality managers compared with its competitors? Are its managers focused on the right objectives? Is the business dependent on attracting and retaining people with hard-to-find skills?

Business Definition. The managers in the business may have an erroneous concept of what the business should be and may consequently target a market that is too narrow or broad, or they may employ too much or too little vertical integration. The trend of outsourcing and alliances is changing the definitions of many businesses, thus creating new parenting opportunities. Is each business in the portfolio defined to maximize its competitive advantage?

Predictable Errors. Does the nature of a business and its situation lead managers to make predictable mistakes? For example, attachment to previous decisions may prevent openness to new alternatives; business maturity often leads to excessive diversification;

long product cycles can encourage excessive reliance on old products; and cyclical markets can lead to over investment during the upswing.

Linkages. Could the business link more effectively with other businesses to improve efficiency or market position? Are linkages among units complex or difficult to establish without parental help?

Common Capabilities. Does the business have capabilities that could be shared among businesses?

Special Expertise. Could the business benefit from specialized or rare expertise that the parent possesses?

External Relations. Does the business have external stakeholders, such as shareholders, government, unions, and suppliers, that the parent company could manage better than it does?

Major Decisions. Does the business face difficult decisions in areas in which it lacks expertise—for example, entering China, making a big acquisition, or dramatically extending capacity? Would the business experience difficulty getting funding for major investments from external capital providers?

Major Changes. Does the business need to make major changes in areas with which its management has little experience?

Understanding the Parent

TO UNDERSTAND THE PARENT ORGANIZATION, we recommend a systematic review of its characteristics in five categories:

- The parent's *mental maps* are the values, aspirations, rules of thumb, biases, and success formulas that guide parent managers as they deal with the businesses. Mental maps shape the parent's perception of opportunities to improve business performance. They embody its understanding of different types of businesses. They underlie the knee-jerk reactions and intuitive assumptions of the parent. Usually, they reflect deeply held attitudes and beliefs and are based on managers' personal experiences. A manager with 20 years of experience in commodity chemicals will have very different maps from one who has spent 20 years in fashion retailing.

- The parenting *structures, systems,* and *processes* are the mechanisms through which the parent creates value. The number of layers in the hierarchy, the existence of a matrix, the appointment processes, human resource systems, budgeting and planning processes, capital-approval systems, decision-making structures, transfer-pricing systems, and other coordination or linkage mechanisms are all important aspects of parenting. The design of structures and processes is important, but more particular to each company is how managers interact within the structure or process.

- Corporate *staff departments* and *central resources* should support line management's efforts to create value. Some parents have large central functions, some as few as possible. Resources, such as patents held by the parent, the corporate brand, special government relationships, or access to scarce property or financial assets, can also be important characteristics. The potential for central staffs and resources to create value depends on the circumstances in each business: a large manufacturing-services staff may be helpful for one business but completely unnecessary or damaging for another.

- Parents often create value because they have *people with unique skills*. The parent's mental maps will likely overlap with the expertise in functions and services. Yet neither of those characteristics sufficiently emphasizes the importance of key individuals in parent companies. Some corporate parents are dominated by managers, such as Jack Welch at General Electric or Allen Sheppard at Grand Metropolitan, whose personalities and skills make a critical difference. But a skilled division head or technical director can also be the parent's greatest source of value, provided his or her style, beliefs, and skills address parenting opportunities in the portfolio.

- The *decentralization contract* between parent and business defines which issues the parent normally influences and which it delegates to business managers. It contains the authorization limits, job descriptions, and formal statements of due process. However, it is typically embedded in the culture of the company rather than fully explicit. The decentralization contract should direct the parent's attention toward those business issues to which it has something to contribute and away from those for which its influence is likely to be damaging.

**Originally published in March–April 1995
Reprint 95202**

About the Contributors

MARCUS ALEXANDER is a director of the Ashridge Strategic Management Centre in London, England. His research and teaching are focused on issues of corporate-level strategy and management of the internal and external boundaries of the organization. He also consults internationally on these topics. He has written extensively on multibusiness companies and the evolution of outsourcing and the virtual organization.

ANDREW CAMPBELL is a director of the Ashridge Strategic Management Centre and Visiting Professor at City University in London, England. Previously, he was a fellow in the Centre for Business Strategy at the London Business School and a consultant at McKinsey & Co. He is the coauthor of *Strategies and Styles: The Role of the Centre in Managing Diversified Corporations*, *A Sense of Mission*, *Strategic Synergy*, *Corporate-Level Strategy: Creating Value in the Multibusiness Company* (John Wiley & Sons, 1994), *Breakup!*, *Core Competency-Based Strategy* and *The Collaborative Enterprise: Why Links between Business Units Often Fail and How to Make Them Work* (Perseus Books, 1999).

DAVID J. COLLIS is currently a visiting associate professor in the strategy area at the Yale School of Management and a consultant to several large U.S. and European corporations. His current research is an international comparison of the role of the corporate office in large multibusiness corporations. He is the coauthor, with Cynthia A. Montgomery, of the recent book *Corporate Strategy* and of many articles in periodicals such as the *Harvard Business Review, Strategic Management Journal, European Management Journal,* and in the books *Managing the Multibusiness Company, International Competitiveness,* and *Beyond Free Trade.*

PHILIP EVANS is a senior vice president of The Boston Consulting Group (BCG) in its Boston office, and worldwide coleader of BCG's Media Convergence practice, which focuses on the strategic implications of the economics of information. He writes on business strategy, and is the coauthor of "Strategy and the New Economics of Information" (*Harvard Business Review*), which was awarded a McKinsey Prize, and the forthcoming *Blown to Bits: How the New Economics of Information Transforms Strategy* (HBS Press, 1999).

MICHAEL GOOLD is a director of the Ashridge Strategic Management Centre in London, England, and also runs the Centre's program on strategic decisions. His research interests are concerned with corporate strategy and the management of multibusiness companies. His publications include *The Collaborative Enterprise: Why Links between Business Units Often Fail and How to Make Them Work* (Perseus Books, 1999), *Corporate-Level Strategy: Creating Value in the Multibusiness Company* (John Wiley & Sons, 1994) and *Strategies and Styles: The Role of the Centre in Managing Diversified Corporations.* He was previously a senior research fellow at the London Business School and a vice president with the Boston Consulting Group.

STUART L. HART is Associate Professor of Strategic Management at the University of North Carolina's Kenan-Flagler Business School. Previously, he taught corporate strategy at the University of Michigan Business School and was the founding director of Michigan's Corporate Environmental Management Program. Professor Hart's research interests center on strategy innovation and change. He is particularly interested in the implications of environmentalism and sustainable development for corporate and competitive strategy. He has published over forty papers and authored or edited four books.

TARUN KHANNA is an associate professor at the Harvard Business School. His research focuses on understanding the scope of firms' activities, particularly the corporate strategy of diversified business groups in several emerging economies of South and East Asia and Latin America. He has written several articles on these subjects and on the structuring and management of licenses and joint ventures, and has served as a consultant to firms in several industries on related issues. He is the author of *Foundations of Neural Networks* (Addison-Wesley, 1989).

KENNETH LIEBERTHAL is William Davidson Professor of Business Administration and is also Professor of Political Science at the University of Michigan, where he has been on the faculty since 1983. Professor Lieberthal has published about a dozen books and more than five dozen articles, mostly focused on Chinese politics and economic decision making. He is currently on leave from the University of Michigan while serving in Washington, D.C., as Special Assistant to the President and Senior Director for Asia on the National Security Council.

CYNTHIA A. MONTGOMERY is the Timken Professor of Business Administration at the Harvard Business School. She focuses her research on corporate strategy and the competitiveness of diversified firms, particularly on issues relating to the markets in which multibusiness firms compete, the resource bases of the firms, and the creation of value across multiple lines of business. She is the coauthor, with David J. Collis, of *Corporate Strategy*; the editor of both *Resource-Based and Evolutionary Theories of the Firm* and, with Michael E. Porter, *Strategy: Seeking and Securing Competitive Advantage*; and the author of numerous articles in management journals. Professor Montgomery is on the board of directors of UNUM Corporation, Newell Co., and several Merrill Lynch mutual funds.

KRISHNA PALEPU is the Ross Graham Walker Professor of Business Administration at the Harvard Business School and a consultant to a wide variety of businesses. His research focuses on analyzing firms' business strategies and the process through which the effectiveness of these strategies is communicated to investors. He has published numerous research papers and teaching cases on these issues and is the coauthor of *Business Analysis and Valuation: Text and Cases*, which won the American Accounting Association's Wildman Award. Professor Palepu is also an associate editor of several leading research journals and is on the boards of Global Trust Bank and Satyam Sparc Solutions.

C.K. PRAHALAD is the Harvey C. Fruehauf Professor of Business Administration at the University of Michigan Business School. His research focuses on the role of and the value added to top management in large diversified, multinational corporations, and he has consulted with numerous firms worldwide. Mr. Prahalad is the coauthor, with Gary Hamel, of *Competing for the Future*, named by *Business Week* as one of the year's best management books in 1994. He is also the author of many award-winning articles, such as "Strategic Intent" and "The Core Competence of the Corporation," which won McKinsey Prizes in 1989 and 1990, respectively.

LAWRENCE E. SHULMAN is a senior vice president and director of The Boston Consulting Group (BCG) in Chicago. He joined BCG in 1979, after completing the MBA program at Harvard Business School, where he was a Baker Scholar.

GEORGE STALK is a senior vice president of The Boston Consulting Group (BCG) and focuses his professional practice on international and time-based competition. He speaks regularly to business and industry associations on time-based competition and other topics. Based in Toronto, he has served as a consultant to a variety of leading manufacturing, retailing, and technology and consumer-oriented companies. Mr. Stalk is the coauthor of the critically acclaimed *Competing Across Time* and *Kaisha: The Japanese Corporation*; his articles have appeared in numerous business publications.

Index

Motorola, 104, 116

multibusiness companies. *See* resource-based strate- gies; synergy, pursuit of

multinational corporations (MNCs), 95–119. *See also* emerging markets

business model for emerg- ing markets and, 99–107

distribution systems and, 105, 107–109

factors in competition for, 98

imperialist mind-set of, 96–98, 116

leadership of, 109–112

local partners and, 113–114, 115, 158–159

politics and, 112–113

transformation of, 115–119

National Tyre Service, 225

nature's economy, 128–129, 133–134

Newell Company

competitive advantage and, 55–56, 57

corporate advantage and, 5, 7–13, 15, 18, 20, 23, 25, 28

Nirma (Indian company), 106, 107

Nirula's (Indian company), 102

Nucor Corporation, 51

oil industry, 209–211

operating control, *vs.* financial control, 30–31

opportunity costs, 65, 70–72, 80

organization

creation of capabilities- based strategy and, 190–191

organizational capabilities as resource and, 36–37, 179, 185, 199, 203–204

parenting framework and, 223, 238

resource-based strategies and, 9–12, 15–18, 19–21

PACE Membership Ware- house, 195

packaging, 105–106

parenting advantage, 208

parenting bias, 63, 69–72

parenting framework, 205–239

benefits of, 234–236

changes in parenting and, 233–234

changes to improve fit and, 226–233

concept of fit and, 209–211

critical success factors and, 212–213

fit assessment and, 211–221

fit at BTR and, 221–226

food company case and, 213, 214, 226–233

mental maps and, 217, 237–239

parent characteristics and, 217–221, 222–223